Adventures in
Edible Plant Foraging

Adventures in
Edible Plant Foraging

Finding, Identifying, Harvesting, and
Preparing Native and Invasive Wild Plants

KAREN MONGER

Skyhorse Publishing

Skyhorse Publishing books may be purchased in bulk at special discounts for sales promotion, corporate gifts, fund-raising, or educational purposes. Special editions can also be created to specifications. For details, contact the Special Sales Department, Skyhorse Publishing, 307 West 36th Street, 11th Floor, New York, NY 10018 or info@skyhorsepublishing.com.

Skyhorse® and Skyhorse Publishing® are registered trademarks of Skyhorse Publishing, Inc.®, a Delaware corporation.

Visit our website at www.skyhorsepublishing.com.

10 9 8

Library of Congress Cataloging-in-Publication Data is available on file.

Cover design by Jane Sheppard
Cover photo credit: The 3 Foragers

Print ISBN: 978-1-63450-407-2
Ebook ISBN: 978-1-63450-889-6

Printed in China

Table of Contents

Chapter 4: Sustainable and Ethical Harvesting . . . 23

Chapter 5: Tools of a Forager . . . 29

Chapter 6: Foraging Wild Berries and Fruits . . . 35

Chapter 7: Foraging Edible Flowers . . . 87

Chapter 8: Foraging Leaves, Greens, Shoots, Stems, Stalks, and Twigs . . . 111

Chapter 9: Foraging and Digging Roots . . . 167

Chapter 10: Foraging Nuts . . . 184

Chapter 11: Seasonal Checklists . . . 201

Chapter 12: Glossary of Terms . . . 205

Chapter 13: Additional Resources . . . 210

Index . . . 213

CHAPTER 1:

Foraging for Wild Food

Have you ever nibbled a few ripe blackcap raspberries growing around the edge of the lawn when doing yard work? Do your kids know what "sour grass" is, and love to munch on the lemony greens? Did you have a great grandmother who used to pick dandelion leaves for dinner or a favorite uncle who hunted mushrooms in fall that he called *stumpies*? I am betting that even the most nature–phobic people living in a large city have heard about the latest trend of finding your own food in parks, or have seen evidence of wild foods on menus of upscale and trendy restaurants. If so, you already have a little personal experience with wild food foraging.

In the beginning of human history before agriculture, we were all wild food foragers, searching our environment for sustenance, medicine, and natural materials to survive. Now with so many modern conveniences like grocery stores, electronic gadgets, and sturdy homes, our connection to the natural world is often reduced to recreational amusements, or worse, a need to tame our lawns into submission and control the habitats that surround us. We as a civilization have lost touch with understanding and appreciating the wild spaces and plants that we live with, including the value of the potential food source under our feet. A healthy interest in your local landscape can pay off with a rewarding pastime of wild food foraging with your family.

Who are The 3 Foragers?

We are a family of three, living in southeastern New England with a passion for hiking, travel, photography, cooking, nature, and wild

1

edible foods. We have happily managed to combine all of our favor-ite things to do into a fun and fulfilling hobby of wild food foraging. We photograph and blog about our adventures, sharing them online, including some personal stories, lots of photographs, plenty of tested recipes featuring our favorite wild plants and fungi, and our travel experiences. We are still learning new things every time we head out into the wild, which keep us fascinated, enthusiastic, and engaged with the environments we find ourselves exploring.

Karen finding wild grapes

I grew up in a mostly rural area in southeastern Connecticut, surrounded by old farm fields and forests, spending time catching frogs in the pond and picking wild blueberries in the summer heat. After a career in foodservice, I became a stay-at-home mom to our daughter for eight years before venturing back into a part time job with the local schools, so I still get my summers off to spend in the woods. I take care of the writing, recipe development, researching the wild plants and fungi we find, plus the trip planning and laundry.

Robert finds a hen of the woods fungus

Robert is originally from Hungary, and it was his initial curiosity about differences between plants in the United States and Europe that led us to research our local plants, fruits, and herbs. He was looking for a springtime plant that he called *medvehagyma* (which translates as bear onion), that he encountered often as a child in Hungary. After hearing his description of the plant, I guessed he might be talking about ramps, a wild leek, and we went in search of this oniony-garlicky delicacy. We tried to figure out where to find some ramps, and that led to our first attempts to educate ourselves on our local wild foods through books and by walking with experienced mentors and wild food educators. Along the way, we learned that the plant he knew from Hungary was similar to our native ramps, but a different species, so we wanted to become familiar with the wild foods that grow in our current area. Robert is the photographer in our family, and he loves to be out hiking and gathering the plants we use to come up with tasty recipes.

Gillian catches a pumpkinseed on her own fishing pole

Gillian is our daughter, the third forager. Exposing her often to the wild foods we seek has made her a wonderfully educated young naturalist. Kids have an innate curiosity about their environment, and you might be amazed how much they can understand, learn, and remember. She loves the sweet berries and the sour sorrels, the cattail-on-the-cob and salads made with edible flowers. Gillian is the chief recipe taster, a budding fisherwoman, and with her sharp eyes and shorter stature, our best mushroom hunter.

I'll introduce you to some of the easiest to identify wild foods, great for beginners or kids. There are many wild foods I will not cover for several reasons: because they are hard to find, need a lot of preparation, are threatened or endangered, or don't taste that great; these are not survival foods, but wild foods to seek for enjoyment. I will be avoiding many of the look-alikes to potentially dangerous plants whose identifications should be left to more experienced foragers. I'll also try to focus on delicious plants that I am fairly certain kids will *love* to eat, and add a few of my family's favorite recipes. All of the wild fruits, berries, nuts, seeds, and greens in this book are foods that my family has eaten and experimented with over the years, and I hope I can convince you that they are worth finding, collecting, and tasting with your family.

Our experiences foraging with Gillian are what inspired this book, and I hope our adventures can motivate you to go out with your own kids, grandchildren, little cousins, and nieces and nephews and enjoy some of the wild foods in your area. Being able to connect with nature using all your senses, including your taste buds, is guaranteed to bring happy memories and full tummies to all wild food adventurers.

CHAPTER 2:

Why Wild Food?

The reasons to get outside with your family and actively hunt for wild berries, fruits, greens, nuts, and fungi are varied. Children, and even inquisitive adults will all benefit from time spent closely observing and tasting a new array of yummy, free, and nutritious wild food. Spending time together participating in active learning strengthens our appreciation for the environment around us, often filling us with wonder and amazement. Creating personal experiences with wild food also teaches awareness of a place, and nurtures an attitude of conservation within children and their caregivers alike. Many of us now have hectic working hours, and children have school, scheduled activities, or spend a good amount of their time playing video games or

Gillian and Robert dig sassafras roots

watching TV, and we have lost touch with the natural world around us. Foraging over several seasons, and eventually years in a favorite spot puts us back in touch with the cyclical patterns of life.

Historically, children often accompanied their elders when they went out to gather wild foods, learning and absorbing the knowledge first hand. Wild food foraging together as a family is one small way to get everyone back outside to actively participate in appreciating new flavors and observing the beauty and blessings of our surroundings. Getting outside and foraging is also *fun*, and you can encourage kids by making it a scavenger or treasure hunt, where the reward is edible!

Delicious and Unique Flavors

Garlic mustard falafel stuffed in pita, with a side of garlic mustard hummus

One reason we continue to seek out and experiment with many wild foods is that they taste wonderful! Even though we live in a small city with three large grocery stores nearby, we often prefer the wild produce we can find ourselves. Many people try to describe the flavors of common wild foods by saying "It tastes like . . .", but we find most wild foods have their own special taste, with fleeting comparison to commercially harvested produce. Wild strawberries may be small in size, but their flavor is so much sweeter, more fragrant, and more intense than their large, watery, cultivated cousins found at the market. Japanese knotweed is often compared to rhubarb or green apples, but all we can say is that it tastes like Japanese knotweed and appreciate it for its own characteristics. Wild foods often offer new tastes and textures, and seeing them offered by chefs on menus at upscale restaurants is becoming more common.

Wineberry Bavarian, a decadent dessert!

Not every new flavor will satisfy all palates, but I still encourage several tries of any new wild food. Often the key to unlocking the best qualities of foraged wild food is knowing *when* to gather the correct parts of the plant, and *how* to properly prepare what you have brought home. Many people have heard that cattails are edible, but if they went out and gathered the seed head in the fall (you know, the part that looks like a hotdog on a stick) and took a big bite of it raw, they might conclude that cattails are awful, and never want to try them again.

They might not be willing to try the tender shoots in mid-spring, the immature flower heads in the late spring that can be boiled and eaten like corn-on-the-cob, or attempt to collect some of the brilliant yellow, nutritious pollen from the male flower in early summer to add to pancakes and smoothies. Knowing the correct season for harvest, careful collection of edible plant parts, and using suggested cooking techniques will optimize the flavor of any wild foraged foods.

Gillian nibbles on some lemony wood sorrel

Children especially love sour flavors, and are surprisingly willing to taste some of the bitter greens. Any recipe they make with greens they picked themselves from the wild become so much more appealing than the spinach you pulled out of the refrigerator. Berries are another

favorite with their sweetness, abundance, and ease of collection for little fingers. Garnishing salads, desserts, or any plate with edible flowers
seems whimsical and slightly magical to kids. By just adding a little bit
of a new, wild food to a familiar favorite recipe, you can incorporate
new tastes slowly.

Chinese pancakes made with wild ramps greens

Harvesting and eating many wild foraged foods is a very immediate, seasonal thing unless you can find ways to preserve your harvests.
Before modern conveniences like supermarkets that sell unseasonal
produce all year, our ancestors gathered and preserved all their food in
warmer months for use in the cold winters. We use several techniques
to put up wild foods and enjoy their flavors all year long. Freezing
lightly blanched wild greens is often the best way to keep them, and
we have kept nettles, dandelion, and garlic mustard successfully. Many
berries will also keep in the freezer, if you can stop yourself from
eating them fresh! Making jelly or jams from berries and fruits is a
wonderful way to preserve the sweet tastes of warmer days. Pickling is
another way to save your harvests for later consumption. Many herbs,

mushrooms, and roots can be dried for long-term storage, used later in the winter for warming herbal tisanes and hearty soups. Eating food that you have gathered yourself and preserved provides a sense of satisfaction and independence all year long.

If It's Free, It's Good for Me

Simply stated, foraging for wild food can save you some money on your food budget. I am not suggesting you and your family to attempt to live only on foraged plants, but by adding them to your diet, you will reduce your grocery bill. Often you will forage for food close to your home, and reduce your carbon footprint in the process. Becoming familiar with your environment insures you won't need to travel far to find a wide assortment of wild foods to easily add to your meals. Many wild foods are simply overlooked, but are easily harvested as vegetables from your garden, and some are even the "weeds" you are pulling and throwing out from your garden!

Yogurt, granola, and wild berry breakfast parfait with blackberries, wineberries, and huckleberries

Two of the best cost reducing examples are berries and greens. Gallons of blackberries can be picked from a field edge in a couple of hours for *free*, versus what you would pay for a pint of blackberries from the supermarket, flown in from some South American country sometime last week. Many wild greens can be used like commercial baby spinach in favorite recipes. Lamb's quarters and nettles are mild enough to substitute for spinach in equal amounts, and some sour or bitter greens like dandelion or dock can be substituted in smaller amounts, all for free. Learning the common wild edibles in your area also gives you a sense of security and self-reliance in unsure times and unstable economies. Your diet can easily be supplemented with free food, if you have the knowledge.

Eating Wild is Eating for Your Health

Adding wild foods to your diet is an easy way to create a more diverse and nutritious way of eating for you and your family. There is a growing body of evidence that wild plants are usually more nutritious than their cultivated counterparts, which have been bred for size, mild flavor, uniformity, long storage, and ease of transport. Disagreeable characteristics like bitterness, sourness, or astringency have been

Gillian holds the still-sheathed cattail flower stalks

reduced through commercial hybridization, which has also reduced the amount of certain vitamins, minerals, and phytochemicals available in our food.

Consider also that wild foods are *wild*; they are grown without commercial fertilizers, pesticides, herbicides, and fungicides, in their natural environment. Wild plants are not grown in depleted soils or in monocultures that are susceptible to diseases and infestations. The wild food you forage for yourself is likely also fresher than food you can buy in the market. We try to take only what we can comfortably eat as soon as possible, unless we have a plan for preservation for a larger harvest. Chances are that you and your family will be out harvesting near your home, which allows for an immediate and local harvest of produce and fungi that are at their peak growing conditions, reducing the loss of vitamins through deterioration and wilting.

Finally, if you are getting outside and walking through a forest or fields to find something to add to your dinner plate, you are outside breathing fresh air and moving. Being out with our daughter has been a priority for us since she was born and we take every opportunity to do so. We vacation in places where we can hike and experience new environments as well as relax, and we make a point of getting outside in good weather as often as our schedules allow us. I can say with confidence that we eat at least one wild food or wild mushroom every day, because wild food foraging has become second nature for my family. Becoming a wild food forager takes practice, and the more often you can get outside, the easier it will be to recognize favorite edibles and just gather a few berries or greens for a meal without a lot of effort.

CHAPTER 3:

Keeping Wild Food Foraging Fun and Safe

Gillian nibbles on a wild carrot

We have been out in the woods hunting wild foods since Gillian was a small baby, often strapped to a carrier on our backs while we hiked. As we were participating in guided foraging tours led by teachers, we would hand her samples of the plant being discussed and always encouraged her to taste what we tasted. As she got older, she began recognizing favorite plants and berries, but we still had her ask us if it is OK to eat something before popping it into her mouth. Now at age 10, she is a confident forager, sometimes to her detriment. I have had teachers at her school tell me Gillian is eating plants on the playground, and parents of her friends have become alarmed when she tries to get her buddies to indulge in the landscape with her! As with any hobby we participate in with our kids, from using a helmet while biking to correctly identifying plants while foraging, there are ways to go about it a safe manner. It will be up to the parents, guardians, or responsible adults to determine whether a child has an ability to engage in foraging in a safe manner, or has the competence and drive to learn these skills. As with other pastimes, active participation by both adults and children will bring about the most success, as it has for my family.

Rule #1

When going out to forage wild foods for the first time with kids, make sure they understand they should not eat *anything* they find without asking a competent and knowledgeable adult first. I know they will be excited to find edible plants, and you may be excited to find some too, but *never eat any part of any plant that you have not identified with 100% certainty*. Overenthusiasm and hasty identification may lead to wishful thinking, where you really, *really* want to find a certain edible plant, and have found something that *sort-of, kinda* looks like that edible plant, but you can be incorrect with unfortunate consequences. *When in doubt, throw it out!* Make sure you have the correct plant, harvest it at the correct time, and prepare it in the correct manner to keep you and your family safe.

Start with information

Each person will have a different way of learning that is best for them. Kids like our daughter Gillian tend to be kinesthetic learners, preferring a hands-on, physical lesson with a bit of visual and auditory information added. Many adults also learn faster by having an experienced teacher or mentor with them in the field to give lessons and provide immediate feedback to questions. I prefer to read a book, and have managed to put together a personal library of more than fifty books about wild food, mushrooms, and foraging non-fiction and memoirs. Robert is a very visual learner, using his camera to capture images to use as a starting point for further research. For most people, kids included, a very effective way to learn the edible plants are to take foraging walks with an experienced teacher.

We are fortunate to have several excellent wild food teachers in our area, and we make a point of walking with them through all the seasons to learn different edibles. Each teacher will have a different personality and focus in their lessons.

Books and identifications guides on wild plants and fungi are becoming more plentiful, and finding the correct resource is important. Try to pick up a book that is specific to your region, as the plants of the Southwest are very different from those growing in New England. Also try to find a guide that is suited to your interests, such as medical uses of plants, a cook book using wild food, a book aimed at families, or a book that shares lore and history of the traditions of foraging. Some identification guides are very specific and extensively focus on only berries or greens, others are very broad, offering less information about more plants. As a book-worm, I like to collect all kinds of books and help support fellow foragers and wild food educators. Owning a book that you can reference often is a way to keep information at your fingertips, and refer to any time you need to look something up. I often add notes to my many books regarding personal observations I have made in the field, and use them as a checklist for the plants and fungi we have observed and eaten.

The internet is becoming an important source of information. There are numerous foraging and fungi identification groups on Facebook offering advice, feedback, and pictures. Blogs can be great sources of information as well. As more people become interested in the many delights and benefits of wild food foraging, the availability of information has grown and offered numerous opportunities for teachers and learners alike.

Move Along at Your Own Pace

When we first became aware of the possibilities of eating wild plants in our area, we were very excited and maybe a little too ambitious. We attempted to learn it all at once and were overwhelmed by the varieties of edibles. Now one of the first pieces of advice I give is to move along at your own pace, and really take your time to build personal relationships with each edible plant or mushroom. Many of our favorite plants have multiple edible parts available in different seasons, so you can't really learn all you want to know about wild food in a day, you need to spend an entire year becoming familiar with the seasonal aspects of an individual plant. Focus on a few wild foods you are really interested in and watch them flower in spring, grow in summer, and produce fruit, seeds, or nuts later in the season. This way you can recognize plants when they are not producing an edible part, and keep in mind of the time of year you should return to harvest. Keeping your learning progress modest also allows you to avoid confusing edible plants with other, potentially non-edible plants because you are trying to do too much at once.

Another reason to start slow is to consider food sensitivities, allergies, and dietary interactions. Try just a little bit of any new food at a time to test your body's reaction. We have a friend who can't tolerate any milkweed, one of our favorites. I personally have found out the hard way that I can't eat daylily flower buds without spending an evening in the bathroom. Kids especially, with their smaller body mass, should restrict their sampling to one new thing at a time. In case there is an adverse reaction ranging from minor flatulence to vomiting or an allergic reaction, you will know which plant or mushroom to avoid in the future. Consider any medications you are taking may interact with a new food as well.

Know Where to Forage, and Where *Not* to Forage

We get asked a lot where we go hunting for wild foods and mushrooms. While a seasoned forager would never give up their "spots", I can give you a few ideas and suggestions on where you should be hunting, and areas you should avoid.

If you have a back yard or garden at your home, you have a fantastic starting point for your foraging adventures. Many of the "weeds" you may be pulling from your flower beds or mowing in the front lawn are actually edible foods. Several wild edible plants love to grow in disturbed soils, like the garden you just tilled up for spring planting. Even in the small tomato patch we grow at our apartment in a raised bed we can harvest purslane, violets, chickweed, wild garlic, lamb's quarters, wood sorrel, red clovers, and common mallow long before the tomatoes ripen. The area of your yard that butts up against a fence or the woods is also a great place to find edibles that like partial shade but will be missed by the lawnmower, and usually lots of berries will grow in this spot. Stepping outside your front door to pick a few wild greens for dinner or berries for dessert is incredibly satisfying and environmentally friendly since you didn't have to drive anywhere to make a meal. The only reasons to *not* be foraging in your own yard are that you have pets that use the yard as their toilet, or you actively spray chemicals like pesticides, herbicides, fertilizers, or fungicides. If your lawn is too small or you use chemicals, consider visiting neighbors, relatives, or friends, checking out their property, and asking permission to gather some wild plants. Likely they will be curious about what you are eating and you might spark some foraging interests within them as well! If you are a member of a community garden or a CSA (Community Supported Agriculture) farm that is organic, consider asking permission to help "weed". Often there are fallow fields or a compost pile that support great populations of edible plants that most farmers won't bother with.

Even in a fairly dense city, you can find untended lots where opportunistic edible plants have managed to grow wild. The field margins of the local baseball or soccer field are often teeming with brushy growth from wild vines and berry bushes. Open spaces like greens in urban and suburban parks often are surrounded by overgrown edges that support both sun-loving and shade-loving plants. Parking lots of small shopping centers may be landscaped with ornamental trees, originally planted for their pretty spring flowers and compact growth. In the late summer or autumn many of those flowering trees will produce fruit like cherries, plums, or crab apples. It is good foraging etiquette to ask permission from the property owners before gathering fruits from their lots. You can explain that you are just harvesting the fruit or berries and it will not damage their landscaping. Some small cities will even plant these fruit-bearing trees along the sidewalks, and then you will be participating in *urban gleaning* when you gather a small basket of free fruit that would have otherwise ended up on the ground. Use common sense and avoid heavily trafficked spots and areas where dogs are likely to do their business.

In more rural settings, roadside foraging can be quite good. In low-traffic areas and especially along dirt roads, you can find fruits, nuts, and berries that might just need a rinse to remove road dust. The shoulders of the road are often considered public areas, but don't stop in an area that is obviously someone's property, and try to stop in areas where you can park safely. Finding abandoned farmland with feral fruit trees and open fields is an option out in the back country areas, but be aware of trespassing laws and toxic chemicals used in industrial farming in the past. I wouldn't recommend foraging along a busy road, due to car exhaust and water runoff contamination. A general rule is to keep about 50 feet from the road to avoid most pollutants, and use your best judgment to determine if roadside foraging is a good idea in your location. Along railroad tracks and under power lines are two places to avoid completely because those areas are often kept open and weed-free with poisonous herbicides and other harmful chemicals.

Foraging in local, state, or federal parks might seem like a good idea, but usually there are regulations against harvesting wild plants. Check with rangers or land managers about rules for particular parks, there is no single law for foraging on all public lands or in public parks. Sometimes there is a limit, like a pint of berries or pound of wild mushrooms per person. Please be respectful and follow all posted rules; often in places like conservation land or sanctuaries there is absolutely no wild food or plant gathering allowed. If you do have permission to forage, or there are rules that do allow foraging in a public place, try to gather the wild food in an out-of-the-way place. While picking berries or a few mushrooms won't deface the beauty of the outdoors for others, digging roots or picking flowers on well-traveled paths is discourteous for fellow hikers in the area who are just out to enjoy the scenery.

The coastal shorelines and inland shorelines are overlooked areas for wild food foraging. Seashores are generally considered public property up to the high tide line; don't trespass on private beaches and land. While visiting the ocean, you can gather seemingly exotic and slightly salty things like seaweeds and glasswort, and small salt-tolerant beach plums. Rugosa roses produce nutritious fruits called the "hips" than can be *carefully* gathered in abundance (thorns!) and you can often find bayberry which has leaves that can be used as a spice like commercial bay leaves. Along inland fresh water bodies, cattails can be abundant, and many berry bushes and small fruit trees will flourish near a year-round water source. If you are gathering food near water, it is important to be aware of the general conditions of the water quality. Avoid polluted waterways and busy harbor areas, stagnant water, and coastal areas where high bacterial count warnings have been issued. Ponds or lakes near commercially farmed lands may have large accumulations of pesticides or other chemical runoff and should be avoided as well.

Just about any habitat will support a variety of different edible wild plants. Start by finding and recognizing the plants in an area familiar to you, and eventually you might find yourself examining the wild plants even while visiting a completely foreign environment. When we head out on vacation during the frigid New England winters, it is generally to some warm, tropical location. In the Caribbean and in Hawaii we have foraged and eaten several fruits and flowers from the forests and beaches, exposing ourselves to truly local plants and foods. If you become as captivated by wild food as we have become, you may find your travels more delicious and interesting as you hunt for wild edibles in diverse surroundings.

Steps for Safely Identifying Edible Plants

Identifying plants or fungi can seem difficult at first for children and adults alike in the beginning. Many guides use botanical terms to describe plant growth and characteristics, and with practice, you will come to remember the at-first unfamiliar terms and recognize the plants with ease. It might seem easier to just match up photos or drawings in a book to the plant you want to identify, but the written observations and descriptions must match as well for a safe and definitive ID, especially for something you plan on eating with your family.

Start with a *tentative* identification by locating and observing a plant you may have recalled from an edible plants book. Observe the flowers (if it is flowering), note the leaf shapes and arrangements, whether the plant parts are hairless or finely hairy, pay attention to smell of the various parts of the plant, examine the fruits that may be present, and the habitat in which the specimen grows. Don't try to identify a plant by a single characteristic. Use *multiple* reliable references to help with your identifications. I also recommend trying to find several specimens in an area to compare their growth just in case you have found a deformed or unusual variety of a plant. Only if you are 100% confident that your plant is correctly identified, edible and in the correct stage of growth for consumption, prepare it according to recommendations and sample a little bit to check your individual reaction before eating a good amount.

You may now be excited about finding an edible wild plant, but I urge a bit of caution for beginners and especially for families with children, because sometimes there are look-alikes for common wild edible plants that don't taste good, or are even dangerous or poisonous. I will try to stick to common, safe edibles in this book, and avoid most plants that have dangerous look-alikes that only more experienced foragers should attempt.

I can't stress enough that it takes *time, patience, and practice* to become a competent and confident wild food foraging family. For us, after more than ten years, we are certain that we can identify many of our local wild edible plants. When we travel to other areas of the continental United States, we have enough practice with observation and identification skills to confidently attempt IDs of plants unfamiliar to us using books, by seeking out wild food teachers, and using internet resources. While traveling to tropical destinations we seek out local resources and guides to help us understand and recognize the local edible plants and fruits we may encounter. For my family, our pastime of wild food foraging keeps us constantly interested, satisfied, and delighted with our discoveries in our local woods and while on vacation. I hope you and your family can safely experience the potential rewards of free, nutritious, wild foods as well.

CHAPTER 4:

Sustainable and Ethical Harvesting

As a potential wild food foraging family or individual, you will have the ability to impact your immediate environment, and the choices you make should be governed by a forager's code of ethics. Commercial harvest of wild foods is becoming increasingly popular to keep up with culinary fads and health food trends, often to the detriment of ecosystems and the natural balance of the environment. Unsustainable overharvest reduces plant populations for all foragers, including wild animals that depend on wild plants to live. We are a family of three, and collect just enough wild plants and fungi for our own *personal* use, and would never feel comfortable as vendors of wild harvested foods. Involving your family and educating them in ethical foraging practices will instill within them reverence for the cycle of life in their very own surroundings. Respectful collection ensures that plants will continue to be present to produce more wild foods for subsequent harvests.

Harvesting With an Eye Towards the *Next* Harvest

Collecting the fruit or berries from plants and collecting mushrooms are considered low-impact harvesting methods. The berries, fruit, and nuts of many plants and trees are generally produced in an overabundance as a means of seed dispersal. Mushrooms produce spores instead of seeds, but the idea is the same. Harvesting the "fruiting bodies" of plants and fungi will not affect the main body: the root of the plant, or the underground mycelium of the mushroom. We feel free to gather large amounts of wild berries, fruits, nuts, seeds, and mushrooms, often collecting enough to preserve for later months. Another low-impact form of foraging is collecting a few leaves from a plant to dry for teas or seasoning, leaving most of the plant behind. Any foraging family could not possibly harvest every berry, nut, or mushroom from any environment, but try to make a conscious effort to leave behind some wild food for animals, and to allow the plants to spread their seeds successfully.

An abundant harvest of wineberries

Harvesting other parts of plants, however, may have negative effects on the population, and needs to be done in much smaller amounts. Taking flowers will prevent a plant from making berries or fruit, or from setting nuts or seeds. Flowers are generally used as garnishes and flavor enhancers, so gathering in quantity is often not a consideration. Harvesting the shoots of many plants in the spring will seriously affect the population of plants. Some may recover, but most will not, so try to gather shoots of abundant native species or invasive species of plants. Digging roots and bulbs is considered a lethal collection of most wild plants, and should be practiced sparingly. A few wild plants *do* benefit from thinning of overabundant or crowded roots, and any invasive plants should be wholly removed without guilt. A general rule is not to harvest more than 10% of a wild food from an area even if there is an abundance of the plant. If the local patch is small, pass it by and look for another area from which to gather. Some wild plants are very important to wildlife or insects, like milkweed for Monarch butterflies, so we don't gather more than we need for a meal at one time. Be aware that the respect you show to your foraging environment and to the plants *now* will affect how long and how well you will be able to utilize the area for *future* harvests.

The caterpillars of Monarch butterflies rely on the leaves of milkweed plants as a food source

Invasive vs. Native

Many ecologists would be thrilled if foragers would gather and consume plants that arc *invasive species*. Invasives are non-native plants that were introduced either intentionally with disastrous results or have arrived through natural methods in a recent time period, and are now threatening the historically native plant populations. Invasive plants use several methods to crowd out and displace native plants. They often arrive with no natural enemies in a new area to keep them in check through consumption or natural diseases. Some plants are *alleopathic*, meaning they produce biochemicals to influence the survival, reproduction, and growth of other plants in the area, reducing competition. Invasive plants can be more successful than native plants by flowering and leafing out earlier, thereby shading out the slower-growing native plants. They also tend to reproduce in abundance, producing massive amounts of berries or seeds. Some invasive plants are even hybridizing with and replacing similar native species. Changes in plant community makeup are natural over time, but some invasive species have run rampant and are radically altering native ecosystems in short periods.

Gillian chomps down on a Japanese knotweed shoot

Native plants are the plants that have existed for a long period in an environment. They occur naturally or have slowly adapted to changes. Some native plants occur in limited or unusual environments and can be easily disturbed or displaced. Native plants often have several species of animals or insects that cooperate with or rely on the plant for existence, maintaining a delicate balance and rich biodiversity of life. Collection of native plants is only encouraged if abundant populations exist in any area, but gathering of endangered plants is illegal. It is wise to research the endangered plant species in your area, and help do your part in their protection.

Summer rolls made with finely sliced and invasive Japanese knotweed shoots

We personally try our hardest to consume the common invasive plants in our area while limiting our foraging of native plants. Coming up with ways to eat large amounts of Japanese knotweed and garlic mustard by creating recipes that make you *want* to add them to your diet is one of our favorite things to do. Collecting *all* of the greens, berries, seeds, or roots of invasive species in an area is encouraged to help control the spread of a population. Plants in this book will be labeled as invasive to encourage liberal gathering and utilization.

I   This is an invasive or introduced plant; please collect as much as you can eat

N   This is a native plant; please gather no more than 10-25% of a healthy population

☆   This is a foraging plant superstar with many useful and edible parts

CHAPTER 5:

Tools of a Forager

Sometimes our wild food foraging is a planned activity, and other times we are surprised by a bounty while going about our daily routine. We try to take advantage of any wild food finds by being prepared to harvest while working, hiking, driving, traveling, or just being out and having fun. I hope wild food foraging can eventually become an integral part of your daily practice as well, and with a little advance planning and preparation you'll be ready to reap the rewards when you come across wonderful, wild foods at any time.

What to Carry With You

A knife, small shovel, notebook and pencil, scissors, gloves, and a collecting bag
are tools of a prepared forager

For a planned hike or trip, you will need to carry some supplies to collect and hold the wild food you are going out to harvest. It is also wise to carry a few "extras" for surprises along the way. Many are items you likely have around the house already, some you may need to buy. Most of these tools and supplies are light and shouldn't take up too much space in your shoulder bag, basket, or backpack. Our daughter carries her own bag with her own supplies to keep her interested and engaged in foraging and to bring home her own finds, whether wild food or interesting rocks, and other items she picks up along the way.

✓ A knife or scissors: We carry folding knives clipped to our pockets to cut plants, branches, and mushroom stems; a pair of scissors is safer for kids, and easier to use on smaller plant parts or on thorny plants

✓ Paper bags: Several sizes and bags to collect leaves, flowers, and fungi; use to keep plants separate

✓ Plastic bags: Useful for wet things and dirty roots; zip-top bags or plastic grocery sacks can be used over and over

✓ Hard plastic containers: These are essential for delicate berries; re-use berry containers from store-bought berries, plastic storage containers, or any hard plastic container with a lid like yogurt cups

✓ Small shovel: A small garden trowel works perfectly to dig up roots and tubers

✓ Gloves: Gardening gloves can provide protection from spines and thorns and keep your hands clean while digging for roots

✓ Water: A re-useable bottle filled with water is essential for keeping yourself hydrated, but can also be used to rinse off your dirty hands and the foods you find before you sample them; you can use it to rinse out your mouth if you find some too-tart or bitter foods

✓ Magnifier: Use the magnifier to confirm specific characteristics of plants or fungi for identification; it also is lots of fun for the kids to look at everything they find close-up

✓ Foraging books: You may want to carry a few books with you when you are beginning just in case you spot some interesting plants or berries you may want to try to identify while in the field

✓ Notebook and pencil, camera: Keep notes and personal observations about wild edible plants you encounter; record your location so you can return later; draw the plant or mushroom to help commit them to memory; take lots of photographs of your wild food finds for ID purposes and for personal memories, then start a scrapbook or even a blog!

Paper bags, plastic bags, and hard plastic containers are used
to collect some wild foods

What to Carry In the Car

Most likely in your car trunk you have a few tools for emergencies like jumper cables, a spare tire, blankets, and a first aid kit. For foraging we carry another set of tools in our vehicle for planned excursions and unexpected finds. We have a crate in the car with more of the supplies we carry in the backpacks, this way we can refill the packs if we need to with more paper and plastic bags, hard containers and water.

- ✓ More foraging books: We can't always carry all the ID guides we want, they can get rather heavy, so we keep some back at the car to reference
- ✓ Bug spray: Use insect repellant for mosquitos, ticks, and chiggers; also dress in light colored clothes and tuck long pants into socks to keep ticks off
- ✓ Dry socks and spare shoes: Plan ahead with extras just in case of surprise mud or curious kids in a stream, it stinks to drive home with wet feet

Extra Tools to Have at Home

Extra equipment to preserve and process your harvest includes canning jars, dehydrators, and an ice cream machine

Over the years we have accumulated a few extra and unusual tools to help with our wild food harvests. We don't carry them in our packs but in the car just in case we'll need them. Some are kitchen tools we keep at home to use in preservation of our foods and fungi for later use in the winter months. They are optional and most beginners won't need them, but they will make harvest and preservation easier for enthusiastic foraging families.

- ✓ Basket or hard container that attaches to your waist or around your neck: Either looped through a belt or tied with a string, this allows you to pick wild food with both hands free
- ✓ Tarp: Spread a tarp under a tree or bush loaded with ripe berries or fruit and *shake* the fruit down in quantity, then tip the tarp into a bucket or hard container
- ✓ Machete: Sometimes you'll need to hack through a jungle of thorny berry canes to get the berries and a pocket knife isn't big enough
- ✓ Telescoping hook: This is a hack where Robert attached a big metal hook to a telescoping painter's pole; we use it to gently hook and pull down branches of trees to pick fruits without harming the tree by breaking the branches
- ✓ Dehydrator: Useful for drying leaves for teas, making fruit leathers from wild fruit, and drying mushrooms for storage
- ✓ Ice cream machine: Make your own ice creams and sorbets with wild fruits and berries
- ✓ Blueberry rake: This was splurge, but it *does* help with picking large quantities of wild blueberries in the summer heat. We also use it for huckleberries, and cranberries in autumn; the teeth gently pick the berries and leave most of the leaves behind
- ✓ Food mill: We use ours mostly to remove seeds from berries before making thick jams
- ✓ Canning supplies: Jars, canning water bath, and ingredients like pectin and vinegar; make pickles and jams from your wild

produce that will taste better than anything you can get from the store!

An aluminum blueberry rake is an extravagant purchase used to collect small wild blueberries, huckleberries, and cranberries

Having the supplies you *might* need available when you find the wild plants and fungi you want to gather allows a foraging family to be prepared for any surprises they may encounter. We even make sure there is space in our luggage for several of the essential wild food foraging tools when we are traveling, like plastic containers, bags, and knives.

CHAPTER 6:

Foraging Wild Berries and Fruits

Fruits and berries are the ripened parts of a tree or plant that spread seeds for reproductive purposes. It just so happens that a good amount of them are edible and *delicious*, worth seeking out and harvesting. The inherent sweetness of most fruit and berries endear them to children instantly, and their small hands can make quick work of low bushes of ripe berries. They may eat a good amount of ripe fruit immediately at the trailside, but if you're lucky you'll be able to bring some home for dessert or preservation in jams, fruit leathers, or for the freezer.

When trying to identify fruits and berries, we look at several key parts of the fruit or berry, and also examine parts of the tree or plant from which it is growing. Several berry canes and some fruit trees have thorns or brambles, so you'll need to be careful and wear protective clothing like long sleeves and jeans when picking. It is very important that *all* parts of the identification match the description:

- ✓ Size and color of the ripe fruit or berry- There may be several stages of ripeness at the same time, so look for the largest or ripest specimen to begin identification; most wild fruits and berries are smaller than their cultivated counterparts (such as wild blueberries and strawberries), but still look familiar.
- ✓ Seeds- Many fruits or berries will have a specific number of seeds or pits that differentiate it from a look-alike; the arrangement of the seeds is also an important identifier; some seeds or pits are edible while others should be removed or spit out.
- ✓ Other identifying characteristics- Study the whole fruit to examine its shape; look for the scar where the flower was attached- does it look like a crown or a dimple; check the outside texture- is it smooth or broken up into small globes, is it bumpy or hairy?
- ✓ Look at the whole plant- Check the leaf shapes, the leaf arrangement, how the bark looks, if there are thorns or hairs present, and observe any distinct attributes of the plant or tree from which the ripe berry or fruit is growing to aid your identification.
- ✓ Knowing the approximate seasonality of each ripe fruit or berry is also important when going out to forage.

Use your *complete* observations of the whole plant and its ripe fruits to later recognize the plant or tree while it is not fruiting. That way, you can find potential foraging spots for the future. Most need nothing more than a rinse before eating, and can be eaten raw immediately without cooking or special preparation. Many wild fruits and berries make excellent jams and freeze well for later use. Foraging for ripe fruits and berries is the fastest way to instant gratification in wild food gathering, and a great kid pleaser.

The berries or fruits of these other wild plants are edible as flavorings or useful, but are discussed in more detail in other sections of this book because of additional, more useful parts:

- Bayberries
- Spicebush berries

Feral Fruits and Berries, Plus Urban Gleaning

Crabapples

Many abandoned or feral fruit trees can be found at old farmsteads or in the woods where yard boundaries used to be. Sometimes states will have purchased old farmland many years ago and converted it into a state park that you can visit and spy old fruit trees. Urban gleaning is the act of collecting wild foods from landscaped or deliberately planted and then forgotten plants or trees in cities. Urban gleaning can take place in abandoned lots where you can collect weedy greens, or fruits from trees and shrubs that hang over public sidewalks and walkways. Cities plant fruit trees for landscaping because of their fragrant spring blossoms. The fruit that will fall (which is a great way to spot the trees—look for the fallen fruit on the sidewalks and in parking lots) is overlooked and not harvested in many cases, making a great mess and attracting scavengers. Berry bushes and fruit trees spring up in unexpected places, "planted" by birds and other animals spreading the seeds in their droppings. Berries and grape vines like full sun, and take advantage of field margins and edges of open spaces to grow in abundance. As many feral fruit trees are on private property or in the lots of private businesses, we recommend that you ask for permission to gather the ripe fruits. Often people are happy to have the fruit picked up and taken away before it starts to ferment or attracts animals. Reassure the property owner or manager of a business that you will collect the fruit without harming the trees, and bring along a fruit picker or plan on climbing smaller trees to get the fruit that grows higher up.

Forgotten or feral apple trees still produce fruit that might
be ugly but is still delicious

Apples

Apples of all shapes, colors and sizes can be found in the wild. Often they are trees that had been planted on a farm within the last century and sometimes you can find an abandoned orchard. The apples won't be flawless; there may be worms, rust, spots, deformed apples, and bees will be attracted to the fermenting sugars. Most of these problems are cosmetic and can be cut away, leaving a good portion of the flesh to eat raw or use in recipes, but we avoid the rotten apples or the overly wormy apples. We go camping with friends on Columbus Day weekend up in western Massachusetts at a state park that was formerly an apple orchard. The grassy field in the center of the park is filled with gnarly, old apple trees that are ripe when we arrive, and we spend all weekend picking up and sampling the forgotten and slightly ugly apples, bringing many home to dehydrate, juice into fresh cider, and make applesauce. Another wild apple cousin is the crabapple, a much smaller and non-cultivated version of an apple. They tend to be more tart than planted apples, but still contain lots of pectin and can be eaten raw if you don't mind sour apples. Crabapples are planted as ornamentals in city parks and in parking lots for their pretty flowers in the spring, while the fruit is largely forgotten.

Feral pears are often forgotten orchard plantings and produce ugly, but delicious fruit

Pears

Finding fruit-bearing pear trees is also possible on old farmsteads. Tiny Callery or Bradford pears are planted strictly as ornamentals; their fruit is so small it is not worth the effort to collect them. Feral pears will be unattractive, lumpy, sometimes with worm holes and rotten spots, and smaller than their tended cousins in orchards, but you can peel the ugly skins and use them in the same ways as purchased pears. Some feral varieties are very firm and take well to canning in a sugar syrup, or make excellent fruit leather. We have friends who allow us to come pick untended pears "out back" in the forest behind their house that has regrown around the pear trees planted in the past.

Sometimes ornamental varieties or fancy varieties of stonefruit can be planted, like these Rainier cherries

Cherries

Cherry trees that grow full-sized cherries are another fruit tree that is usually planted for its pretty spring blossoms rather than its fruit. At a local elementary school, a Rainier cherry tree was planted in honor of a past principal. We were dropping Gillian off to catch a bus to summer camp when I wondered why the birds were making such a ruckus in one of the trees, and noticed it was full of ripe, yellow cherries! I contacted the school's principal and got her blessing to collect 3 gallons of beautiful cherries that day, making pies, and eating them raw all week. By asking permission, I was able to collect some free, delicious fruit that would have otherwise gone to waste.

Plums

We encounter these trees planted as ornamental landscaping in parking lots or along city streets less often than other fruit trees. The harvest is small, sometimes just a few fruits, and they are generally not very good since the tree has been hybridized more for its showy flowers and compact growth.

Autumn Olive, Silverberry I

Elaeagnus umbellata

This is not an olive at all, but an invasive fruit that can be incredibly abundant. Kids will love the sweet-sour flavor, and adults will appreciate the nutritional benefits.

Autumn olive berries

How to Identify

Autumn olives are perennial shrubs that often grow in dense thickets of scraggly looking bushes, up to fifteen feet tall. The entire plant, including the ripe berries, has a silvery appearance. The leaves grow alternately on short stems and are elliptic, tapering at both ends; have wavy but untoothed edges, and the undersides are lighter green. Autumn olives are one of the earliest shrubs to flower in the spring; the fragrant flowers are white to yellow, hang from the leaf axils, and have four petals joined at their bases to form a tube. The fruits are oval to round drupes, ripening to red, about ⅓ inch long, and covered with silver speckles. Each fruit contains a single, elongated, soft seed that is lined along its length; chewing and swallowing the edible seed is optional, although I prefer to spit them out.

Ripe autumn olive berries and their fibrous but nutritious seeds are
full of essential fatty acids

Habitat and Range

Autumn olive shrubs grow in open woodlands, grassy areas, abandoned fields, waste grounds, and along roadsides. Their roots fix nitrogen, changing the soil composition, and allow it to grow in areas with poor soil. Autumn olives grow best in full sun, but will tolerate some shade. They range from the central plains of Nebraska, through the upper Midwest, the Northeast into Canada, along Eastern North America into the South, and in Washington state and Oregon. They are originally from Asia and had been erroneously planted as erosion barriers and roadside foliage before their destructive spreading potential was discovered. They are classified as invasive, noxious weeds in several states. Feel free to harvest as many berries as you can to slow the spread of this invasive plant!

When and How to Harvest

Autumn olive fruits become ripe in late summer, continue to ripen throughout the autumn, and may persist after the first frosts. The fruits should be red and plump when fully ripe, and we have found that each individual bush's fruit has its own flavor characteristics—some are very sweet while others are prohibitively astringent, so taste a few before harvesting. They are easily pulled from their short stems and can be gathered in great quantities over a tarp or bucket.

Eating and Preserving

Kids will happily eat these fruits raw from the bush. Autumn olives get their brilliant red color from lycopenes, a phytonutrient thought to fight some cancers and reduce the risk of cardiovascular disease; the fruits contain 13-16 times the lycopenes of fresh tomatoes. We run them through the food mill to remove the seeds which results in a thick, red pulp that we sweeten and use to make jams, dips and dressings, wine, dessert sauces, and fruit leather. The raw, whole fruits also freeze well. We were inspired by their similarity to tomatoes, so we made ketchup from the ripe autumn olive fruits.

Autumn olive Ketchup   Tomato Ketchup

Autumn Olive Ketchup

Makes about ½ cup

3 cups raw autumn olives
1 tablespoon white wine vinegar
½ teaspoon salt
3 Tablespoons raw sugar
¼ teaspoon allspice
2 cloves of garlic, crushed

1. Add the raw autumn olives to a saucepan with 2 Tablespoons water. Cook over medium heat 5 minutes, stirring, until the berries have burst. Press the pulp through a fine sieve or food mill to remove the seeds and small stems. You will end up with about 1 cup of puree.

2. Cook the puree for 5 minutes over medium heat, until the color darkens.

3. Place the puree in a blender with the vinegar, salt, sugar, allspice, and crushed garlic, and pulse a few times to smooth out the puree.

4. Return the ketchup to the saucepan and cook over low heat to reduce further. Cook for about 10 minutes, stirring often, until it is thick like ketchup. Taste and add more salt as needed. Store covered in the refrigerator.

Beach Plums N

Prunus maritima

Summertime is beach time with the kids, and wild food foragers can make it plum-picking time for the whole family.

Beach plum flowers and ripe fruit

How to Identify

Beach plums are deciduous shrubs, growing four to eight feet tall. The leaves are alternate and elliptic, have serrated edges, and are a lighter green on the undersides. The bark of the twigs is reddish-brown while the main trunk is grey with bark that flakes off in large pieces. In May, the trees flower profusely; often the branches are covered in white, five-petaled flowers. The fruit is a drupe with a single, hard pit inside which should be removed before eating or spit out. The plum looks similar to cultivated plums, but is much smaller, only up to one inch in diameter. They ripen to a dark purple or blue, and will be slightly soft. The fruit is often covered with a white, powdery coating which can be rubbed off; the coating is just a layer of natural wax that keeps the fruit from drying out.

Habitat and Range

Beach plum shrubs are salt-tolerant and grow along sandy beaches on the Atlantic coast from Maine south to Maryland. They prefer full sun and well-drained soil. Beach plums are native to North America, and have historically been collected and consumed by colonists in jams and preserves. Harvesting beach plums will not harm the shrubs as long as you don't break their branches off.

When and How to Harvest

Beach plums ripen in late August and early September. Not all plums will ripen at the same time, so more than one trip to the beach for harvest is possible. You will want the darkest purple or blue plums, not the reddish ones that are still very hard. The ripe plums hang from a short stem from the undersides of the branches, so it may be difficult to see them at first without moving the leaves aside. In August, we take the ferry from New London, Connecticut over to Long Island to meet some friends and forage for the beach plums that line the shores. In past years, we have easily filled coolers full of the small, tart plums, and spend evenings pitting plums for jams and recipes. We handpick

Summer cobbler made from pitted beach plums

these into hard containers, keeping in mind that the pit is about one third of the volume of the fruit, so you'll need a few gallons to bring home enough for multiple recipes.

Eating and Preserving

The ripe fruits of beach plums are wonderful eaten raw while spending time at the beach. The skin is tart, while the rosy flesh is sweet and fruity, creating an ideal balance of flavors; and they are perfectly kid-sized by nature! Beach plums are high in vitamin A and contain natural pectin; making them a great candidate for jam with the pits removed but the skins on for a chunky spread. We pit these easily by hand, and use the plums in cakes, ice cream, dehydrated like raisins, made into fruit leather, preserves, infused liqueurs, and baked into fruit cobblers.

Blackberries I, N

Rubus species

Found in almost all parts of the planet in many different forms, the instantly recognizable blackberry is a safe edible to identify and eat; they are only hazardous to pick due to the brambles!

Blackberry flowers and fruits

Blackberry canes

How to Identify

These biennial, woody shrubs produce only leaves in their first year of growth on lighter-colored upright canes; they produce leaves, flowers and fruit in their second year in dense thickets of darker-colored and tougher canes. Another species of blackberry, called dewberries, grow on a ground-hugging vine-like shrub. Their leaves are compound, toothed, and coarsely textured with pointed tips; the terminal leaflet is larger than the side leaflets and up to 5 inches long. Blackberry canes have brambles, or thorns, and their "ouch-factor" varies greatly between the many species. Blackberries produce white, five-petaled flowers in April. The berries are aggregate fruits, meaning many drupelets are connected together and there is one small, hard, edible seed inside each globule. When ripe, the receptacle (white core) remains inside the picked berry, making it appear solid; fully ripe berries are glossy and purplish-black, appearing similar to cultivated varieties available at the supermarket. There are no poisonous berries that look like any of the species of blackberries.

Dewberries tend to trail their thorny brambles along the ground

Habitat and Range

Blackberries prefer full sun and often grow at the edges of fields and in disturbed areas. They grow in temperate zones all across the United States and globally. There are several native species, as well as invasive species; sometimes telling the difference is difficult but not important to a forager since they are all edible to different degrees. Regional names for different varieties of blackberries include boysenberry, marionberry, loganberry, and brambleberry. Gathering blackberries and their cousins, whether native or invasive, will not harm the plant since they spread through underground runners and the large amount of seeds.

When and How to Harvest

In most areas, blackberries ripen in mid to late summer, which presents a dilemma for foragers: It is very hot and humid outside, but you need to wear jeans, long sleeves, and boots to protect yourself from the relentless thorns of the blackberry canes. We go out picking in the very early morning hours, before the heat becomes unbearable, and then come home and shower. This is one item we forage using a machete, sometimes making tunnels through the head-high canes into the center of the thicket. Using a hands free method of holding your collection container is preferable for picking thorny blackberries as you can use one hand to hold on to the plant and keep its brambles under control, while using the other hand to pick the berries. We use a plastic container-lined basket tied to our waists, and we can just lift out the plastic container when it is full and replace it with another empty plastic container to keep picking. Small amounts encountered while out hiking are best picked into shallow, hard containers to prevent crushing the delicate berries. The berries do not all ripen at once, so you'll be able to make several trips out to the berry patch to collect ripe berries.

Eating and Preserving

Fresh blackberries are delicious to eat raw while taking a hike. The ripe fruit is rich in antioxidants, dietary fiber, and vitamin C. We like them in yogurt or sprinkled over cereal for breakfast, baked into cobblers or pies, and juiced and added to lemonade or made into a fruity mousse. Making jams and jellies are traditional uses, and we use a food mill to remove the seeds for a thick, pulpy jam. Blackberries freeze well using the IQF method of preservation, or their seedless juice can be frozen in containers.

Blueberries and Huckleberries N

Vaccinium species and Gaylussacia species
One of the first berries I learned to recognize as a child, wild blueberries, is still a favorite fruit in our house. Wild blueberries are smaller but often more intensely flavored than their cultivated cousins, a welcome addition to the berry abundances of summer.

The pretty bell-shaped flowers and fruit of wild blueberries

Is this a blueberry or a huckleberry?

While wild blueberries and huckleberries are from different plant genera, they appear enough alike that people often use their common names interchangeably. To make it more confusing, there are more than twenty different varieties of wild blueberries: most commonly encountered are the low-bush blueberry (*Vaccinium augustufolium*), the high-bush blueberry (*Vaccinium corymbosum*) and a velvet-leaf blueberry (*Vaccinium myrtilloides*). Huckleberries are from another genus of small shrubs, *Gaylussacia,* and there are eight different species of huckleberries that grow throughout North America. *The berries of both blueberry and huckleberry bushes are equally edible.* The easiest way to tell the difference between wild blueberries and huckleberries is to look at the seeds. Carefully slice an unripe or under-ripe berry in half around its equator. Wild blueberries have many, tiny seeds scattered throughout the berry. Huckleberries will have about 10 larger seeds (botanically, they are *nutlets*) arranged in a circle inside the berry. Huckleberries also have golden resin dots visible on the backsides of their leaves, and the leaves can sometimes be pressed onto a piece of paper or the back of your hand to leave behind a golden image in the outline of the leaf.

Huckleberries   Blueberries

How to Identify

Both wild blueberries and huckleberries have similar appearances, with a few variations in height, and leaf shape and size. They are small trees or low-growing shrubs with alternate, oval leaves that taper at both ends and are smooth or finely toothed; the leaves are slightly wooly in some species. In the northern areas of North America, the leaves are deciduous and turn a brilliant red in autumn before dropping. Their height can range from six inches to fourteen feet tall, depending on the species. In spring, both shrubs produce small white to pink, bell-shaped flowers with four or five short petals, growing in clusters on short stems. The berries start off green and ripen to a blackish-blue, often coated with a whitish powder which is a natural wax that the plant produces to prevent the berry from drying out. (It is not necessary to remove the whitish bloom from the berries before they are eaten.) Wild blueberries and huckleberries will have a 5-parted crown on the bottom of the berry, which is a key identification characteristic.

Habitat and Range

Wild blueberries and huckleberries prefer poor, acidic soil. They are native to North America, but harvesting wild blueberries or huckleberries will not harm their population. They can reproduce through underground rhizomes, so there are often large thickets of shrubs in an area. They grow throughout the upper Midwest to Texas, east to New England and eastern Canada, and throughout the South, with an area of growth in the Pacific Northwest and California as well. Wild blueberries are the official fruit of Maine.

When and How to Harvest

Wild blueberries and huckleberries start to ripen in July and can still be found at the end of August. They are best picked by hand into hard plastic containers. The little fingers of kids are the best tools for this, although you might not get too many berries in the container since they will all go straight into their mouths! Finding a fully laden high-bush blueberry tree is a blessing for your back, since you won't have to stoop over to pick berries. Blueberry rakes are another option if you find yourself surrounded by lots of berries every year, but are not necessary for the casual forager.

Breakfast smoothie made from wild blueberries and bananas

Eating and Preserving

Sun warmed wild blueberries and huckleberries are perfect raw, eating as you go along. Wild blueberries are high in vitamin C and manganese, and contain anthocyanins, powerful anti-oxidants thought to help prevent heart disease. They contain some pectin and make wonderfully thick jams. If you are fortunate to come across a large amount, they can be frozen IQF style. Spread washed and dried berries on a parchment paper-lined cookie sheet in the freezer, and when they have frozen solid, scoop them into a plastic bag for storage. For cooking, huckleberries will produce a "crunchier" product due to the slightly larger nutlets. We don't make pies from wild blueberries because there are too many skins and seeds to make an appetizing full-sized pie, but make a thickened pie-like filling for sweet, yeast-raised dough or use puff pastry to make turnovers for breakfast.

Chokecherries and Black Cherries N

Prunus serotina, Prunus virginiana
With tastes ranging from tart and sour to astringent, wild cherries may seem undesirable compared to their cultivated cousins. Their abundant availability and transformation through cooking into jams and syrups are what make them worth seeking out.

Leaves and fruit of wild cherries, (inset) flowers of wild cherries

How to Identify

Wild cherry trees can grow up to ninety feet high, but will produce fruit on much smaller trees. The bark of wild cherries is reddish-brown or grey when young, covered with lenticels that grow in horizontal lines. The older bark is dark grey and rough, looking like flaky, craggy blocks. The leaves of black cherries are alternate, glossy ovals with tapered bases and pointed tips, finely toothed, and have fine, reddish hairs on the underside of the leaf along the midrib. Leaves of chokecherries are similarly shaped as black cherry tree leaves, but wider and lacking the hairs on the leaf midrib. Scratching the tender bark from the twigs will produce a noticeable bitter almond scent. The flowers bloom in mid-spring; they are 5 petaled, white, and grow in elongated, drooping racemes. Black cherries are smooth, round drupes with a single pit, about ⅓ inch in diameter, growing in racemes with short, red stemlets. They are opaque and totally black when ripe. Chokecherries grow in a similar raceme, have a single pit, and are red to purplish-red when ripe. The fruits of both wild cherry trees are edible, while the pits should not be chewed or swallowed if broken due to the presence of hydrocyanic acid.

Habitat and Range

Black cherries are considered "pioneer" trees because they are often the first trees to populate open fields along sunny margins of undeveloped areas. They are native to North America, widely dispersed by birds. Picking wild black cherries or chokecherries will not affect their ability to reproduce since there are plenty of cherries for the birds to eat on tall trees that you can't possibly reach. They flourish abundantly in the eastern three-quarters of North America, and in Washington and western Canada.

When and How to Harvest

Black cherries ripen to black in mid to late summer, while chokecherries ripen to dark red in mid-summer. Both varieties grow from the drooping racemes, and you can often run your hand along the main stem to pop off more than one cherry at a time. The pits are large compared to the fruit, so you'll need to collect a large amount of fruit to have enough usable flesh for recipes.

Ripe chokecherries

Eating and Preserving

Black cherries and chokecherries can be eaten raw from the tree. Kids might like the puckery, astringent fruit, but many people will prefer them cooked with sweeteners. Each tree will have its own flavor, so try a few before picking a bucketful from a tree, and remember to spit out the pits. We briefly cook the ripe cherries with a little bit of water then run them through the food mill or a sieve to remove the pits and use the black, pulpy juice for jam, to make sauces for ice cream, or cake fillings. We also mix the juice into syrup for pancakes, or into lemonade for a pretty color and interesting new taste.

Cranberries N

Vaccinium macrocarpon, Vaccinium oxycoccus
Historically important foods for Native Americans and then the Colonists, wild cranberries have changed very little and closely resemble those found at the supermarket.

Flowers of cranberries, wild cranberries on a bush, and some ripe cranberries cut open to show the hollow air pockets

How to Identify

Cranberries are creeping sub-shrubs, vine-like in appearance, growing up to 2 feet in length. The stems are slender, hairless, and slightly woody. The leaves are smooth, hairless, and evergreen, growing alternately. Leaves of small cranberry (*V. oxycoccus*) are less than 3/8 inch long, have pointed tips, rolled edges, and are white on the underside. Leaves of the large cranberry (*V. macrocarpon*) are ¼ to ¾ inch long, narrowly oval with blunt tips, with flat edges, and they are pale green on the underside. The flowers of both cranberries appear similar, with four pink petals that turn straight back and yellow stamens that are bundled together pointing downward, looking similar to a crane's bill. The fruits grow from thin, wiry stems from leaf axils along the stem. The berries may be ½ inch in diameter, looking comically large compared to the tiny leaves, and bear a strong resemblance to commercially cultivated cranberries. They ripen from pale green to red. There are three or four hollow air chambers inside the ripe berry, and they have many tiny, light brown, edible seeds embedded in the spongy, white flesh.

Habitat and Range

Wild cranberries are found in wet, acidic areas such as fens, Pine Barrens, and sphagnum bogs, sometimes very near coastal areas protected by sand dunes. They do not live submerged in water, but can tolerate some periods of flooding. They are native plants and range from Minnesota, down through the high-altitude mountains of Tennessee, along the east coast into New England and the eastern provinces of Canada. They also grow on the west coast from California north through Alaska. Cranberries are a major commercial crop for Massachusetts, New Jersey, Oregon, and Wisconsin. Harvesting the ripe fruit gently from the plants will not harm the plant population as they spread mainly through underground rhizomes.

When and How to Harvest

Cranberries begin to ripen in some areas in late summer, and you may be able to prolong the harvest until the first snows of winter. The berries can persist through the winter, and we have visited our cranberry patch in late winter to find softer but still edible red berries on the plants. The berries should be mostly red when ripe, but may be mottled with white. When gathering ripe cranberries by hand, we pick into buckets. They are very light due to their large air chamber and the spongy, white insides, and will readily float. Their skins are tougher than most berries, so you can put a large volume in one bucket without damaging the harvest. We are able to collect large quantities in a short time by using our blueberry rake; in the past it was somewhat back-breaking work to bend over or squat down and hand pick the berries from the low-growing plants; being shorter, Gillian still likes to pick cranberries by hand.

Eating and Preserving

Fresh cranberries are very tart and not often eaten raw, although kids may enjoy them for their ultra-sour zing. Wild cranberries are rich in anti-oxidants and high in pectin. Cranberry-orange-walnut muffins are a favorite breakfast treat in our house. We juice cranberries and add sweetener, or cook them into a chunky cranberry sauce for holidays. Wild cranberries can be dehydrated, but will not be sweet and pliable like the ones you can buy; they will be drier and more tart. Cranberries freeze fantastically by spreading a layer on a cookie sheet, freezing, and then bagging the hard berries for long term storage.

Cranberry-Orange-Nut Muffins
Makes about 12

2¼ cup unbleached flour
½ cup sugar
½ teaspoon salt
1 teaspoon baking powder
½ teaspoon baking soda
Zest of 1 orange
1 cup buttermilk
2 large eggs
¼ cup oil or melted butter
Juice of 1 orange (about 3 tablespoons)
1 cup halved cranberries
½ cup chopped nuts (we like walnuts or hickory nuts)

1. Heat the oven to 400°F. Line a muffin tin with muffin papers or butter and flour the muffin tin.

2. In a large bowl, combine the flour, sugar, salt, baking powder, baking soda, and orange zest.

3. In a smaller bowl, whisk together the buttermilk, eggs, oil, and orange juice.

4. Using a spoon, gently mix the wet ingredients into the dry ingredients, stirring as little as possible; there should still be a few lumps. Fold in the cranberries and nuts.

5. Scoop into the muffin pan, and bake for 10 minutes. Lower the heat to 350°F and continue baking for 10-15 minutes longer until the tops spring back when lightly pressed. Cool.

Grapes N ☆

Vitus sp.

With several edible parts, wide distribution, and often delicious fruit, wild grapes are a useful addition to a foraging family's list of edibles.

Tender tendrils, leaves, and ripe grapes

How to Identify

Wild grapes grow on a perennial, woody vine (botanically, it is actually a liana) that can be up to fifty feet long; the older growth has shaggy brown bark while the younger growth is green and flexible. Grapes use forked, tender tendrils to wrap around other trees or plants to climb high into the tree tops in search of sunshine; each tendril grows on the vine opposite from a leaf. The leaves can vary between the dozen or so wild species growing in North America; most are large, often toothed, and can have 3 or 5 lobes that can be shallow or deep, sometimes finely downy on the undersides. The grapes grow in a tight cluster hanging from the vine on a sturdy stem, opposite a leaf, on short stemlets. The size of the ripe fruit ranges from ½ inch to ¾ inch in diameter, and the larger grape varieties are generally better tasting. Grapes have several edible seeds inside their translucent pulp, usually 2-5 per grape. Their skins ripen to a purplish-black, often coated with a harmless white bloom of natural wax the grape produces to retain moisture.

Note: With so many possible variations in the leaves and the colors and sizes of ripe grapes, it is important that three key characteristics are present to verify identification and not confuse wild grapes with several poisonous look-alikes such as Canada moonseed, Virginia creeper, or porcelainberry. *Grapes must have tendrils, multiple seeds per berry, and a woody vine.*

Habitat and Range

Grape vines prefer full sun, and they will climb anything in their search for it. They are often found on riverbanks, edges of fields, woodland margins, and thickets. Different species of wild grapes are present throughout all of North America, with the fox grape (*Vitus labrusca*), the riverbank grape (*Vitus riparia*), and the muscadine (*Vitus rotundifolia*) being the best tasting. Picking grapes in large quantities will not harm the vines. Many wild animals love grapes, and plenty will be left behind higher up.

When and How to Harvest

Wild grapes have several edible parts that can be gathered at different times. Leaves can be picked in the spring before the veins become too tough, but the leaves have grown large enough to stuff. Don't strip a vine; rather pick one or two leaves from each. The tender, forked tendrils are a favorite of Gillian's; we call them monkey tails, and she picks them in the summer and chews on them for a tangy, sour treat. The grapes themselves ripen in late summer and autumn, and I usually smell them before I can see them. Use scissors or clippers to snip off the whole cluster of ripe grapes rather than picking each one individually, and clean and de-stem them when you get home. We pick them directly into five gallon buckets that sit at our feet, and the long-handled hook we have works well to pull the higher grapes down to reach.

Eating and Preserving

The young leaves can be poached, stuffed with grains, rolled up, and steamed for the freshest and tastiest stuffed grape leaves you have ever eaten. Many folks who make their own pickles swear that adding a grape leaf to the jar will keep the pickles crunchier. Gillian always has a fistful of sour monkey tails (the tender tendrils) to nibble as we hike. The ripe grapes make excellent juice with a little sweetener added. The skins of grapes contain resveratrol, an antioxidant thought to prevent high cholesterol and prevent blood clots. Wild grapes also contain B vitamins and natural anti-inflammatory phytochemicals. Wild grapes have varying levels of tartrate that will cause irritation of your skin or mouth if ingested, so you need to let the fresh juice rest until the tartrates sink to the bottom of the container in a thick sludge, then pour off the juice without disturbing the settled layer of tartrates. We make jam from the larger and sweeter fox grapes we find; it has an incredibly rich flavor, much better than anything you could ever buy at the supermarket.

Mulberries N, I

Morus alba, Morus nigra, Morus rubra
Resembling blackberries at a quick glance, mulberries grow from trees. The berries are easy to collect in quantity, but may leave you with purple-stained fingers for a few days.

A branch heavy with ripe and unripe mulberries

How to Identify

There are three primary species of mulberries that can be found in different parts of the continental United States: white, black, and red mulberries. Their exact botanical identification is not critical as they are all equally edible. Mulberries are medium trees, growing up to sixty feet tall. The bark of older trees is brown and ridged, and white mulberry trees have orange colored areas between the ridges. The leaves are very variable; some may have irregular lobes, some may be heart shaped, leaf edges may have rounded teeth or pointed teeth, and they grow alternately on the branches. The fruit hangs from a short stem that stays attached to the berry once picked. Each globule of the aggregate fruit has a conspicuous black dot on the outside and one small, edible seed. The different species of mulberries ripen to different colors, the red and black taste best when ripened to a dark purplish-black, and the white mulberry will often have a purple or pink tint to it when fully ripe.

Habitat and Range

Mulberry trees are found in woodlands, fields, and along city streets. Black mulberries are primarily a southern tree, the red mulberry grows in the eastern half of the US, and the white mulberry grows throughout the country. White and black mulberries are non-native species, and the white mulberry is considered an invasive pest in the Northeast and Wisconsin; red mulberries are native to North America. Harvesting the fruit will not impact the tree population; they are spread far and wide by birds and you couldn't possibly reach or pick all of the ripe berries.

When and How to Harvest

Mulberry fruit ripens in early summer, and not all the fruit ripens at once, allowing for multiple harvests. We often first notice the location of trees when the ripe fruit drops to the ground or sidewalk, making a large purple stain. They are collected by placing a tarp or bed sheet under the tree and shaking the branches, the ripe fruit will fall easily.

Eating and Preserving

Mulberries are delicious eaten raw, although the white variety is less juicy. We make jam and tarts using mulberries, and add them to morning smoothies. They are one of the earliest berries to ripen in quantity, and we eat as many as we can in season.

Black and White Mulberry Ricotta Tart
One 10" tart

Crust:
1¼ cups cookie crumbs
3 Tablespoons sugar
5 Tablespoons melted butter

Filling:
15 oz. container whole milk ricotta
7 Tablespoons sugar
3 Tablespoons flour
2 egg yolks
1 teaspoon lemon zest (about 1 lemon)
pinch of salt
2 egg whites
1½ cups mixed mulberries, washed

1. Make the crumb crust by mixing the crumbs with the sugar and melted butter. Press into a 10" tart pan. Heat the oven to 325° F.
2. With a wooden spoon, mix the ricotta with the flour and sugar until well blended.

3. Add the egg yolks, lemon zest and pinch of salt and mix until combined.

4. Whip the egg whites to soft peaks, then fold them into the ricotta mixture gently. Pour into prepared tart crust.

5. Top the tart with the mulberries, pressing them gently into the batter. I snipped the stems off, but it is not required.

6. Bake for 30-38 minutes. The filling will puff up, but still move a bit in the center. Cool and refrigerate.

Partridgeberries N

Mitchella repens
While partridgeberries don't have much flavor, they seem to be a favorite for kids to find and eat while out in the woods, and can even be found in winter when there is not much else to see.

A ripe partridgeberry, notice the two "eyes" at the bottom

How to Identify

Partridgeberries are creeping, ground-hugging evergreen plants that are often less than two inches in height, but forms mats covering large areas of the forest floor as the stems can grow up to three feet long. Their long, leathery stems have deep green leaves that are broad at the base and taper to a rounded point, and are ½ to ¾ inch long. The leaves grow in opposite pairs, and have a lighter colored mid rib and light yellowish undersides. They flower in late June, and have a white, 4 petaled double flower that is fused at its base to form a single berry. The berry ripens to red, will have two small dimples on the underside where the flowers were attached and many small, brown, edible seeds inside the white, mealy interior.

Habitat and Range

Partridgeberries grow in mixed deciduous and evergreen forests. They prefer rich, acidic soil, and can carpet large areas with their pretty foliage. They grow east from Minnesota and Texas to the coast, up into eastern Canada, and south into Florida. They are native to North America, and harvesting the berries will not harm the plants, but be sure to leave some behind for wildlife like birds, rodents, and other small mammals to find in the winter.

When and How to Harvest

The fruit of the partridgeberry plant ripens to red in September and can persist on the plant through the winter and still be harvested into the following spring. We hand pick them into a hard plastic container.

Eating and Preserving

The taste of ripe partridgeberries is mildly sweet, but often described as bland. Kids love to find them and eat them while hiking, spotting the red berries in late autumn, during mild winter days when there is a little bit of snow cover, and in the springtime when there is not much else to find. We also add them to a salad for color. It is not really practical to try to find enough for long term storage.

Raspberries and Black Raspberries N

Rubus strigosus, Rubus occidentalis
Two of the native raspberries we have in North America, these berries are easy to identify and are real kid and crowd pleasers in taste.

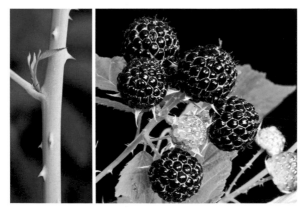

Powdery canes and berries of black raspberry

How to Identify

Both raspberry varieties grow on woody canes that only bear flowers and fruit in their second year. The canes of red raspberries (*Rubus strigosus*) are erect instead of arching, light green to tan and covered with thorns. The leaves consist of three to seven toothed, oval leaflets; the flowers of raspberries are five-petaled and white. The black raspberry (*Rubus occidentalis*) canes are also thorny, but distinctly arching and covered with a greenish-blue powdery bloom than can be easily rubbed off. Their leaves consist of three to five doubly toothed leaflets, and are white on the undersides; their flowers are five-petaled and white, with noticeably longer sepals in the center. The berries are compound aggregate fruits, meaning many drupelets are connected together and there is one small, hard, edible seed inside each globule. When ripe and picked, the white core (the receptacle) is left behind on the calyx, leaving the berry hollow. Raspberries ripen to red, while black raspberries ripen from red to black and should only be picked when black. There are no poisonous berries that look like raspberries or black raspberries.

Habitat and Range

Raspberries and black raspberries grow in full or partial sunlight, often at the edges of fields, on hillsides, along roadsides, and near fresh water. Both species are native to North America, with the raspberry found throughout the entire country and black raspberry is found in the eastern two-thirds of the country. Harvesting the berries will not cause harm to the plants as their seeds are prolifically spread by birds. The plants also reproduce when the arching canes take root as they contact the ground.

When and How to Harvest

Black raspberries ripen first, in late June. They should be very dark purple or almost black before being picked. They will not even come off from the plant if they are not fully ripe, so don't try to pull them off, they should release easily. Raspberries ripen later in mid-summer. Both berries are easily picked in large quantities by little children's fingers if they can avoid the brambles and stop eating them immediately. Pick them into shallow, hard plastic containers as they are delicate and will squish easily.

Wild red raspberries

Eating and Preserving

We often eat these gems fresh in some yogurt or in breakfast smoothies, or they can be made into jams or jellies to preserve the taste of summer. Use them in stunning desserts the same way you use store-bought raspberries, but feel good about not paying store prices for the beautiful fruit. Both berries contain vitamin C, and fiber. Ripe black raspberries also contain high levels of anthocyanins, which are antioxidants. Raspberries and black raspberries are a favorite of adults and children alike, and an afternoon spent picking from the wild berry patch is an afternoon well spent.

Rosehips I, N

Rosa rugosa, Rosa carolina, Rosa virginiana, Rosa species
Hybridized by gardeners for their showy flowers and smell, roses are a popular cultivated plant. Wild roses can be foraged for their fruit, the hips, and the fragrant flower petals can be consumed as well, making them another useful plant for a foraging family.

Wild rugosa beach roses and their large hips

How to Identify

Wild roses grow as bushy, multi-stemmed shrubs, sometimes as vine-like brambles with arching canes. The older growth of the canes is woody and prickly, while the newer growth is green and tender, but will still bear plenty of prickles. The leaves are compound with three to eleven oval toothed leaflets, growing alternately on the cane, some-times with lighter and finely-hairy undersides. The flowers are large but showy, but simple; with five petals ranging in color from white to pink, five sepals under the flower that persist on the ripe hips, and multiple yellow stamens and pistils. The hips form beneath the flower, swelling as the flower matures and the petals fall to the ground, then getting larger as the season progresses and finally ripening to orange or red. The larger the hips, the more flesh you will get to eat because they are often filled with many hard, hairy seed-like achenes that are edible, but quite bitter. The ripe hips range in size from ¼ inch to over

1 inch in diameter, are oval or round, and have the withered five-petaled sepal still attached to the end.

Habitat and Range

There are many native wild roses in North America, like *Rosa virginiana* and *Rosa carolina*, that grow in clearings and along field margins, in sunny woodlands, and along lakes and rivers from the Midwest to the East Coast. Other native varieties like *Rosa californica* grow along the West Coast. One invasive rose and our favorite rosehip to harvest is the beach rose, *Rosa rugosa*, which can tolerate salty coastal areas of the East Coast from Canada south to Virginia, and Washington and Alaska. Another invasive rose, *Rosa multiflora*, grows in the eastern 2/3 of North America, as well as the west coast, but produces the smallest and seediest hip, making it almost useless as a foraged food. Collecting the flower petals or the mature hips from the plants will not harm the wild rose populations, but other woodland animals use the ripe hips as food throughout the winter, spreading the seeds through their scat.

When and How to Harvest

Most varieties of wild roses flower in the summer, and we gather the fragrant flower petals in the morning because they will wilt and fall off the plant by late afternoon. We just gently tug the petals off into a paper bag, as they are delicate but slightly succulent, and picking them into plastic bags will make them deteriorate quickly. The hips ripen in late summer through the autumn, and can persist on the shrubs through the first frosts, after which the flesh surrounding the seeds will be sweeter and softer. Sometimes the hips can be a bit prickly, so we use gardening gloves to pop them off their stems into buckets, or use scissors to snip them.

Eating and Preserving

The delicate and fragrant flowers can be eaten raw in salads, preserved in honey, dried for teas, or made into floral syrups. Depending on the

A warm herbal tisane can be made from dehydrated rosehips

species of wild roses you encounter, the amount of the sweet flesh on the hip varies. We slice them open to scrape out the hairy, bitter seeds, and then use the flesh cooked and pureed like applesauce, or cook them down further to make rose hip butter. The cleaned rosehips also make a pretty, pink jelly, and dehydrate well for use in the winter. Gillian likes to eat the ripe rosehips raw when we are at the beach; they taste a little like fresh apricots. Ripe rosehips are high in vitamin C, vitamin E, niacin, and beta carotene.

Small but delicious wild strawberries

Strawberries N

Fragaria virginiana, Fragaria vesca

Looking like a miniature version of our cultivated, store-bought strawberries, the wild strawberry is much more intensely flavored. Kids will love to search for the ripe, red jewels hidden under leaves in large patches, eating most of them warmed by the early summer sunshine.

How to Identify

Wild strawberries are low, herbaceous perennials that look very similar to cultivated strawberry plants. Their leaves are divided into three, coarsely toothed leaflets that are 1-3 inches in length, usually covered in fine hairs on the underside. The flowers are produced on hairy stalks that grow directly from the ground, in loose clusters of two to ten flowers with 5 white petals and many yellow stamens in the center. Once pollinated, the fruit will grow and ripen to red in about five weeks. The ripe fruit is heart shaped and will often have the calyx and stem attached when picked. The woodland strawberry (*Fragaria vesca*) has its small, edible seeds resting on the surface of the berry, while the smaller Virginia wild strawberry (*Fragaria virginiana*) has its edible seeds depressed into the flesh of the berry. Both varieties are red when ripe. *Look-alike alert*: There is another berry that very closely resembles wild strawberries, called the mock-strawberry (*Duchesnea indica*). Its seeds rest on the outside of the berry flesh like a woodland strawberry, but the flowers of mock-strawberry have yellow petals, the flesh is white and spongy, and the berry is essentially edible but completely flavorless.

Habitat and Range

Wild strawberries are native to North America and widespread in temperate zones. The Virginia strawberry is found in the entire continental United States and throughout Canada, while the woodland strawberry is absent only in the Deep South, desert areas, and Alaska. They prefer well drained soil in full sun to partial shade, and are often found alongside rural or dirt roads, meadows and fields, along streams, and in disturbed areas. They spread through scaly underground rhizomes and by horizontal runners aboveground. Gathering wild strawberries will not impact the population as they often form large patches. The birds also love them, and will help spread their seeds.

When and How to Harvest

Wild strawberries ripen at about the same time as cultivated local berries, in the first few weeks of June, sometimes persisting into July.

Picking wee, wild strawberries can be a time consuming endeavor. The berries are hard to spot without moving the leaves aside but once you find a large patch, have a seat and start picking them into hard plastic containers; the berries are quite juicy and delicate.

Eating and Preserving

Due to their small size, picking enough wild strawberries for recipes is not practical for many adults; it takes a lot of patience and a great patch of berries to collect enough for jam, pureed sauces, fruit leather, or shortcake. For kids, hunting and eating them while spending the afternoon running around outside can be tons of fun and produce wonderful summertime memories of wild foods.

Sumac N

Rhus copallina, Rhus glabra, Rhus typhina
There are several wonderfully edible sumacs in North America, although many people are initially scared off by the word "sumac"; edible sumacs are not the same as poison sumac. Their tartness is attributed to several acids, and they can have culinary uses similar to citrus.

Ripe berries of staghorn, smooth, and winged sumac

How to Identify

Edible sumacs are small trees or large shrubs that grow as dense colonies of clones, generally from 3-15 feet tall. They have pinnately compound leaves that grow alternately and can be 12 to 24 inches long; each with 11 to 13 lance shaped, toothed leaflets 2-5 inches long. When cut, the stems will exude a sticky white sap. The fruits are large, 3-6 inch long cone-shaped clusters of sticky drupes that grow upright at the end of the branches and ripen to various shades of red, reddish-orange and reddish-purple. The three different species have slightly different appearances in berry cluster and leaf appearance. The winged sumac (*Rhus copallina*) has a flared midrib between the leaflets on the leaf stalk, and the smooth berries ripen to a purplish-red. Smooth sumac (*Rhus glabra*) has a smooth and light purple midrib on the leaf stalk, and a looser cluster of smooth berries that ripen to reddish-orange. Staghorn sumac (*Rhus typhina*) has a tan, fuzzy midrib stem, similar to the velvet on a deer's young antlers, and the berries are very tightly clustered and very fuzzy. The foliage of edible sumacs turns a brilliant scarlet in autumn. *Note:* Poison sumac (*Toxicodendron vernix*) also has compound leaves, but they grow in swamps, and the berries are white and grow in drooping racemes.

Notice how the white berries of poison sumac droop down beneath the branches and leaves

Habitat and Range

Edible sumacs grow in fields and at field edges, disturbed areas, along highways, and on waste grounds. Winged and staghorn sumac grow in the eastern half of the United States, while smooth sumac grows in the lower forty-eight states. There are other types of sumac, such as *Rhus trilobata* in the west, and *Rhus lanceolata* in the south that appear similar and can be used in similar ways as the discussed edible sumacs. Sumacs are native plants with historical uses by Native Americans. Harvesting the ripe berry clusters will not affect the growth of the colony, as they spread by underground rhizomes. Birds will also consume the berries and plant sumac through their droppings.

Leaves of staghorn, smooth, and winged sumac

When and How to Harvest

The flowers of sumacs appear as yellow-green conical clusters in early summer, giving way to the clusters of hard berries. The berry clusters of the three common sumacs ripen to red, reddish-orange, or purplish-red at different times in the summer, allowing for an extended harvest of the berry clusters. In our area of New England, first comes the staghorn sumac, and then the smooth sumac, and finally the winged sumac at the tail end of summer and into the early fall. These are not juicy berries to be eaten out of hand; rather you want to use the tart acids on the outer surface of the berries for drinks, jellies, and other recipes. You'll want to avoid collecting the berry clusters after it rains, as all the sour properties will get washed away; in time they may produce enough acids to get sour again. To check for ripeness, we do the "lick test" by either licking the berry cluster directly, or sticking a wet finger into the interior of the cluster and then licking our finger. The flavor will be sour and slightly fruity, similar to lemons or other tart citrus. Collect the entire ripe berry drupe by snipping them off into a bag or bucket to take home. Later in the season the berry clusters can harbor colonies of insects or caterpillars and their feces; you'll want to avoid the bug filled clusters as there is no way to clean them.

A tart sumacade drink can be made with sumac berry clusters

Eating and Preserving

An incredibly refreshing and pretty drink can be easily made from the ripe berry clusters of sumac. It is the malic acid, gallic acid, tannic acid, and small amount of ascorbic acid on the berries that produce the tart drink. Start by breaking up the berry clusters in a pitcher and add cool or room temperature water to soak the clusters; using hot water will bring out too much of the tannic acid and make an unpleasantly bitter and astringent drink. The water will turn a light shade of pink or orange in a couple of hours, depending on the ripeness of the berries and amount used, then strain the drink through a coffee filter to remove any hair from the berries or other debris and sweeten to taste with honey or sugar. To make a stronger concentrate, soak another bunch of berries in the same liquid until the desired strength is reached; the concentrate can then be frozen in ice cube trays and used later. We have also successfully dried the ripe berry clusters in a paper bag, and reconstituted them at a later time for a tart drink. In the Middle East, they have a different sumac variety (*Rhus coriaria*) whose tart berries are ground into a blend of spices called za'atar, usually a mix of sumac, dried oregano, and sesame seeds. We have ground the berries of smooth sumac in a coffee grinder to use in similar ways, as it does not have the irritating hairs of the staghorn sumac berries. I love to use the concentrated sour liquid in recipes in place of lemon juice, in jellies and in a meringue pie recipe.

Sumac Meringue Pie
Makes 8 Ramekins, Or 1-9" Pie

Sumac Curd:
1½ cups sugar
⅓ cup cornstarch
½ cup water
1½ cups sumac concentrate

5 egg yolks
1 Tablespoon butter

Meringue:
5 egg whites
¼ teaspoon cream of tartar
1 cup plus 2 Tablespoons sugar

Par-baked pie crust if making a pie

1. Heat the oven to 375°F.
2. To make the curd, whisk the sugar with the cornstarch in a medium saucepan. Add the water, sumac concentrate, and yolks, and whisk until smooth.
3. Place the pan over medium-high heat and cook slowly, stirring often with a silicone spatula. The curd will thicken, allow it to come to a slow boil for 1 minute then remove it from the heat. Whisk in the butter, and then pour into the ramekins or pie crust.
4. To make the meringue, whip the 5 egg whites with a mixer on medium until frothy. Add the cream of tartar, and whip on high until soft peaks form. Slowly pour in the 1 cup plus 2 T sugar, and continue whipping until stiff peaks form.
5. Scoop the meringue over the hot curd, trying to cover it completely. Bake for 14-18 minutes, until evenly golden brown. Cool, and refrigerate.

Wineberries I

Rubus phoenicolasius

A relative of native raspberries, the glassy appearance of invasive wineberries is as beautiful as it is tasty. Collect wineberries as freely as you desire to create delicious, fruity desserts.

Flowers, the prickly cane covered with sticky bristles, and
ripe fruits of the wineberry

How to Identify

Wineberries resemble native raspberries. The canes are covered in hairy, sticky glandular bristles, but they also contain the characteristic painful prickles of other members of the *Rubus* family. They grow lighter colored green canes in their first year, and the canes darken and produce flowers and the berries in their second year. The leaves are three-parted, toothed, and their undersides are white. The flowers are 5-petaled, white, and grow loosely in clusters on very bristly stems. The orange-red fruits are compound aggregate fruits, meaning many drupelets are connected together and there is one small, hard, edible seed inside each globule. When ripe and picked, the white core (the receptacle) is left behind on the calyx, leaving the berry hollow, similar to a raspberry. Each globule of the ripe wineberry has the appearance of translucent glass. There are no poisonous berries that look like wineberries.

Habitat and Range

Wineberries grow in partial sunlight in large thickets, often at roadsides, edges of fields, and in disturbed areas. They are native to Asia and are considered invasive in the eastern half of the United States, from Illinois and Arkansas through the Northeast and south to Georgia. Harvesting all the ripe wineberries you see will not affect the plant's ability to survive, and is recommended as it is such an invasive plant and is taking over the habitat of the native black raspberry. Wineberries spread through seeds and when the tip of the berry canes arches over and reaches the ground, it will produce roots for new plants.

When and How to Harvest

Wineberries ripen in mid-summer, usually in the hottest months of July and August. You'll still need some protective clothing to enter a wineberry thicket for picking, and count on getting sticky from brushing into the red glandular hairs on the entire plant. Pick wineberries into shallow, hard plastic containers as they can be delicate and squish easily. Using a picking container tied to your neck or waist is very useful, as you can use both hands to protect yourself from the prickles while you gather the berries in quantity.

Eating and Preserving

We think wineberries have a perfect balance of sweet and tart. They make incredibly beautiful, red jams once we run them through the food mill to remove the seeds. The pulp is useful for making fruit mousses and as an ice cream topping. Whole wineberries freeze well using the IQF method, and then we use them in oatmeal, muffins, or smoothies all year around. Wineberries contain vitamin C, antioxidants, minerals and fiber, and are a great addition to any forager's berry list.

Wintergreen N

Gaultheria procumbens
Known as wintergreen, teaberry, or checkerberry, this refreshingly minty plant is a delight to find and chew as an instant breath freshener.

The pretty bell-shaped flower leathery foliage, and fruit of wintergreen berry

How to Identify

Wintergreen is a ground hugging, evergreen, trailing subshrub. Their dark green leaves are leathery and shiny, oval shaped with a pointy tip, about 1 to 2 inches long, have a lighter colored midrib and underside, and are hairless. They grow alternately on a woody stem that runs just under the surface of the ground, connecting several plants in a colony. Wintergreen flowers in mid-summer, producing white, bell-shaped flowers with five short lobes that hang downward from the uppermost leaf axil. The berries ripen to red in late fall, with a star-like split on the bottom of the ripe berry. The berry is not juicy, but has white, mealy insides with many, very small edible seeds. The leaves and berries have a wonderful wintergreen smell and flavor when chewed or crushed.

Habitat and Range

Wintergreen grows in mixed or conifer forests in the eastern half of North America, into higher elevations in the southern states, and north through Canada. It prefers light shade and can be found in sphagnum bogs, sandy soil, and clearings in the forest. Wintergreen is native to North America, and while there are many low-growing plants that are called some version of wintergreen, only *Gaultheria procumbens* has a minty smell and taste. Harvesting the berries and a few leaves from a large colony of wintergreen will not harm the plant.

When and How to Harvest

The evergreen leaves of wintergreen can be gently plucked or snipped off of the woody stem all year long. The new spring leaves will be lighter green and less leathery, and some leaves may have a red tinge, but they are still fine to eat. Don't take more than 10-25 percent of the leaves from a patch of wintergreen. The berries are good to harvest once they turn red and they will persist on the plant even under snow cover from late fall through the following spring in good shape. The berries can be gathered in quantity, but try to leave a few for the wildlife to find during a cold winter.

Eating and Preserving

The leathery leaves of wintergreen can be chewed as a breath freshener, but should be spit out and not swallowed. The berries can be chewed and swallowed with no problems. Kids will love this natural "gum" that they can find out in the woods to chew. A refreshing herbal tisane can be made from steeping the crushed fresh leaves in warm or room temperature water for a few hours. The volatile oils that give wintergreen its flavor will dissipate quickly if you boil the tisane, and some people like to lightly ferment the steeped liquid to extract more of the wintergreen oils. Methyl salicylate is the source of the wintergreen flavor and is closely related to the compound found in aspirin. A strong infusion of wintergreen is not only tasty, but it has a mild ability to sooth sore throats, reduce fever, and relieve minor aches and headaches. The leaves are available year-round to pick fresh, so we don't dry them since they will lose their minty flavor. The fresh berries can be added to smoothies for a minty kick, but the flavor will be diminished if you try to dehydrate them. I was able to gather enough berries one spring that had made it through the winter to bring some crispy meringue cookies to a wild foods potluck, where they all disappeared!

Wintergreen Meringue Cookies
Makes about 48

1 cup fresh wintergreen berries
4 egg whites, room temperature
½ teaspoon cream of tartar
1 cups sugar

1. In a food processor, chop the wintergreen berries into a coarse paste, scraping down the sides of the processor bowl. You will end up with about 4 Tablespoons of a dry paste.
2. Preheat the oven to 250° F.
3. In a mixer bowl, whip the egg whites until foamy. Add the cream of tartar, and then continue to whip to soft peaks.

4. Slowly add the sugar, and mix the egg whites until they form stiff peaks. With a whisk, mix in the wintergreen berry puree by hand, trying not to deflate the whipped egg whites.

5. Using a large star tip, pipe out the meringue into rosettes, leaving about ½" between each meringue. Bake for 3 hours until dry and crisp. Store the meringues in an airtight container.

CHAPTER 7:

Foraging Edible Flowers

Flowers are the reproductive parts of plants and trees. They can be fragrant and beautiful, and civilizations have attributed symbolic meanings onto many of them. Flowers have been inspirational in works of art, featured at festivals, parts of religious ceremonies, and the stars at botanical gardens worldwide. Gifts of flowers are given at important life events; at births, graduations, weddings, and even funerals, flowers play a prominent role because of their agreeable appearance. If you grow a garden, you know that the flowers of your vegetables need to be pollinated by bees or insects in order for your vegetables to grow successfully. Did you know that some of your vegetables are actually the flower themselves, like broccoli, cauliflower, and artichokes? As a wild food forager, you will see flowers as the precursors to future fruits and vegetables or seeds that a plant disperses, and you will see many of them as a food source on their own. Kids will love the delicate and colorful blooms you add to salads, lending an imaginative air to mealtimes. The herbal tisanes and floral syrups made from fragrant flowers are caffeine-free and safe for kids to drink, and the jewel-like jellies make for fanciful sandwiches. Snacking on flowers while walking with your family seems whimsical, and kids will really enjoy eating the sweet and charming treats they can find while outside.

The collection of flowers for eating is considered a non-lethal form of foraging for the plant. You will likely not harm or kill the plant or tree from which you are collecting, however you will be limiting the future fruit, nut, or seed production of the plant and removing a possible food source for bees and other insects. Overharvest of blossoms is not a large concern when it comes to trees, as the tree is often too tall for you to possibly collect every flower. It may seem like a blessing in disguise when I tell you to go out and harvest flowers of common lawn invaders like dandelion and red clover in large quantities. Remember that you may want to selectively collect blooms that have been planted in gardens or flowers in public places so as not to diminish the esthetic appearances for others.

There are a few safety issues to consider when collecting flowers to consume. You want to make sure your flowers are safe to eat by properly identifying them using the features of the flower as well as the rest of the plant. It is best to avoid collecting from high-traffic areas where many people walk their dogs, and avoid collecting from the immediate roadsides where snow abating chemicals and automobile fumes accumulate. Make yourself aware of any possible chemicals used on lawns or fields from which you want to harvest and stay away from pesticides, fertilizers, herbicides, and other poisons. The last things to watch out for are insect hitchhikers in your blossoms; bees, beetles, caterpillars and spiders can tumble out of your bag along with your flowers and become uninvited guests to dinner, so give the flowers a shake before collection.

Edible flowers can be simply added to fresh salads or used as garnish on meals, or they can be candied, dried and made into herbal tisanes, made into fragrant syrups, added to batters and fried, and cooked in favorite recipes. The most expensive spice in the world, saffron, is collected from a crocus flower, and other flowers are used as flavorings like cloves, hops, and capers. The wild flowers and blooms you collect can add unexpected beauty and floral flavors to your foraged food menus, and a level of playfulness and magic to your food for kids.

The flowers of these other plants are edible, but discussed and identified in more detail in other sections of this book because of their additional, more useful parts:

- Chickweed
- Chicory
- Dandelion
- Garlic mustard
- Roses
- Milkweed

Black Locust N

Robinia pseudoacacia
The clusters of fragrant flowers of the black locust are terrific eaten raw, and they work well in recipes that take advantage of their sweet crunch.

Black locust flower clusters

How to Identify

Black locust blossoms grow on a tree that can be eighty feet tall and has brownish-grey, deeply furrowed bark. The leaves are pinnately compound, 6 to 12 inches long with 7 to 21 toothless, oval leaflets. Pairs of small spines grow from many of the leaf bases. Before the leaves develop in spring, the tree produces racemes of white pea-like flowers which make the whole tree appear white. The flowers have a yellow spot on their upper petal and are very fragrant. Later in the season, the flowers will produce bean-like pods that are 2 to 6 inches long and contain 4 to 7 flat, rounded seeds. The seeds are edible with careful preparation, but we avoid them.

Habitat and Range

Black locusts are native, pioneer trees that will quickly populate unused field edges before other plants move in. They prefer full sun and often grow at roadsides and along edges of rivers and parking lots. They occur throughout all of North America and parts of southern Canada.

Like other members of the legume family, black locust trees have the ability to fix nitrogen in the soil and can tolerate poor soil conditions. Harvesting the clusters of flowers for consumption will not harm the tree; likely you wouldn't be able to reach the flowers that grow very high.

When and How to Harvest

Black locust trees flower very early in the spring season, during the last week of May into the first week of June, and only do so for about two weeks before the flowers wilt and turn brown. We gather the entire flower cluster by pulling it from the lowest hanging branches and collect them into buckets. Some of the blossoms will not be open fully at the bottom of the cluster, but they will still be crunchy and sweet. Avoid the flowers that have already gone brown. They should not be collected immediately after it rains, as the nectar and wonderful smell will have been washed away.

Eating and Preserving

The flowers of the black locust are wonderful eaten raw, and we toss them into our mouths like popcorn. They have a nice crunch and a sweet, honey-like flavor with a mild sweet pea taste. We have added the fragrant blossoms to doughnuts, ice cream, salads, and flavored sugar with the fresh blooms to use in baking. The flowers can be frozen in an air-tight plastic container, but we prefer to eat them fresh in season. *Note*: While the seeds inside the pods are edible, they require some special processing to make them safe. All other parts of the black locust tree are poisonous, including the leaves, leaflets, roots, and inner bark.

Black Locust Flower Doughnuts

Makes about 24

1⅓ cups flour
1½ teaspoons baking powder

¼ teaspoon salt
⅔ cup milk
1 egg
2 cups black locust flowers, green parts removed
Oil for deep frying

1. Heat your oil to 375°.
2. Mix the flour with the baking powder and salt.
3. Beat the egg and add it to the milk. Gently whisk the wet ingredients into the dry ingredients.
4. Fold in the black locust flowers.
5. Fry about 1 Tablespoon of batter for each doughnut, about 30 seconds on each side.
6. Dust with powdered sugar and serve warm.

Cattail N ☆

Typha augustifolia, Typha latifolia

Cattails are often referred to as the "supermarket of the swamps" because of all of their edible parts that are available at different times of their growing season. Our favorite part is the immature pollen-bearing flowers; we eat them like corn-on-the-cob or add the pollen-rich staminate flower parts to recipes.

Cattail flowers and seed heads, the common "hot dog on a stick" that is recognized

How to Identify

Cattails have long, sword-like pointed leaves with parallel veins that grow directly from the rhizomes, which are often growing horizontally underwater or in very wet mud. The flowers grow from a central stalk that is wrapped in a pale green bract, and the male and female portions are separate on the top of the stalk. Once fertilized by the pollen from the upper, male portion of the flower, the lower female portion will produce thousands of fluffy seeds and the immediately recognizable "hot dog". The pollen bearing male portion of the flower will fall away once the pollen is spent. Cattail stands are easy to spot because the old seed heads often overwinter and persist until new flower heads grow.

Habitat and Range

Broadleaf cattail (*Typha latifolia*) is native to North America and found throughout the country. Narrowleaf cattail (*Typha augustifolia*) is an introduced plant from Europe that is now considered naturalized and often found in salty coastal marshes, but also throughout most of the United States. Cattails grow in dense stands in marshes, swamps, ditches, and stagnant water so it is important to be aware of the water quality from which you plan on gathering your cattails. They spread through underground rhizomes and their numerous seeds, so it should not impact a population too much if a forager collects some immature flowers, the early spring shoots or even if you attempt to extract some starch from the fibrous rhizomes.

When and How to Harvest

The starchy rhizomes can be collected any time of year when the water is not too cold to enter; you'll need to get wet to pull them up. While we have read about the procedure to obtain starch from the rhizomes, we have never bothered with the time consuming process for a small yield of starch. Later in the spring when the new growth of leaves are about 3 or 4 feet tall but the flower stalk has not yet formed, you can gather the tender shoots by pulling back the outermost leaves from the center, then pulling the last bunch in the center straight up, yanking out the heart of the plant. Peel back a few of the green leaves until you reach the white core that will snap off cleanly to indicate the tender part you want to eat. The flower stalk appears next in late spring and you'll want to pick it when it is still covered in a pale leaf bract. We find that you can collect the immature flowers for food for a period of two weeks. We cut the whole flower stalk off and take them home to clean by peeling off the bract, then separating the male flower (the top portion) from the female flower (the bottom portion). The pollen of the cattail flowers can be collected in early summer once the upper male portion is mature. It swells up and turns yellow with the nutritious pollen, and can be collected in a couple of ways. We used to cut a hole in the side of a milk jug and bend the pollen-heavy flowers into the jug and shake it around while standing knee-deep in some swamp. Now we just snap off the whole male portion and bring it home to shake out the pollen in a more controlled (and dry) manner. We then sift the pollen through a very fine meshed sieve to remove fibers and little insects. Throughout the growing season you can try to harvest the young growing tips of the rhizomes, another activity that will require you to get wet. Feel along the rhizomes under the surface of the water until you reach an end. If the pointed tip that is growing from the end is not curved towards the water's surface, it will be young and not fibrous like the mature rhizomes. Snap it off, wash to remove the mud, and cook it in soups. The size of the rhizome tips is fairly unimpressive, so we don't bother to collect it anymore.

Pinching off the male flower parts yields a delicious food, and the pollen is sweet and bright yellow

Eating and Preserving

The shoots of the early spring leaves don't last long once we pull some of them up. Gillian loves the mild flavor and will eat them by the dozen. We eat it raw or sliced in stir-fries, and on occasion have gathered enough to lightly pickle. It tastes a bit like cucumber and is commonly called "Cossack's asparagus". To eat the flowers, we cut off the entire stalk and bring it home to peel the bract away. Usually there are many little black beetles hiding under the bract, but they are easily shaken off. We then boil the flowers for three minutes before adding some butter and salt and eating them like corn-on-the-cob. The lower, female portion will not yield very much edible plant material, but you can scrape the flower with your teeth. The male, upper portion contains a good amount of tender fibers that you can bite off easily, leaving a thin, white core behind. After a meal of the male flowers, we are left with a bunch of the cores on a plate, looking like a pile of fish bones! The flavor is fairly reminiscent of sweet corn. We also pinch the raw fibers off the male portion of the flower to cook in soups and batters. We have successfully removed the green flower fibers from the male flower when still raw and stored it in an airtight plastic container in the freezer for a year, taking out and using some when we feel a craving for cattail flower griddlecakes or chowder. We collect the sweet pollen and store it in the freezer as well, using it all year added to make sunshine-yellow biscuits, pancakes, muffins, and smoothies. The pollen contains protein, fat, fiber, calcium, iron, and vitamin C, making it comparable to the expensive pollen you can buy at the local health food store.

Cattails also have many other practical uses in wildcrafting. The dry "hot dogs" make excellent fire starting material in tinder bundles, and fantastic play scepters for imaginative kids. The green leaves can be used to weave mats or thatching on the roof of a play hut or shelter.

Cattail Flower Griddle Cakes

Makes about 12- 2" cakes

2 large eggs
1 Tablespoon milk
2 Tablespoons flour
½ teaspoon baking powder

1 cup cattail flower spike pulp
1 Tablespoon minced sweet red pepper
1 Tablespoon minced glasswort, chopped chives, or field garlic (optional)
½ teaspoon salt
Pinch of pepper

Garnish with sour cream and glasswort, chopped chives, or field garlic

1. Mix the milk, egg, flour and baking powder together with a whisk until no lumps remain.
2. Stir in the remaining ingredients.
3. Cook the batter by tablespoonful on medium-heat griddle, flipping after a minute, until browned on both sides.
4. Allow the cakes to cool, and serve with a dollop of sour cream and more glasswort as garnish.

Daylily I ☆

Hemerocallis fulva

Another wild food forager's favorite because of its multiple edible parts, the common daylily is originally from Asia and has since become naturalized in North America. The flowers are the most showy

Shoots, tubers, flower buds, and mature flowers of daylilies

visible part and edible at three stages, along with the early shoots and the underground tubers.

How to Identify

The perennial daylily plant has long, sword like leaves with paral-lel veins running along the entire length. The leaves are 1 to 3 feet long when fully mature, growing from the base of the stem. The flower stalks are leafless, often much taller than the leaves, and bear 10 to 20 blossoms each. The orange flowers open successively, not all at once, and each flower is only open for one day (hence the name daylily) before wilting and falling to the ground. The flowers are a combination of 3 upper petals and 3 lower sepals, 6 stamens, and one large pistil; it appears as a 6 petaled, orange, funnel-shaped flower. If the plant is not blooming when you find it, you can confirm its identity and differentiate daylilies from similar looking foliage of irises and daffodils by digging up its tubers. The daylily has roots attached to potato-like tubers, while daffodils grow from a single bulb and irises grow from a horizontal rhizome.

Habitat and Range

Daylilies are an introduced species that have escaped cultivation and become naturalized; they range throughout the majority of North America, except for the southwest. They grow in sunny or partially sunny places, along roadsides or around field edges, in disturbed areas, and near homesteads and gardens. Daylilies spread through their underground tubers into large colonies; harvesting the shoots, flowers, or tubers will not harm the plant's population and may help alleviate overcrowding by thinning the colony. They can be invasive, and it is not a good idea to deliberately spread daylilies.

When and How to Harvest

The shoots can be harvested in spring before they grow over 6 inches tall; otherwise they become stringy and acrid. Cut the rosette of the shoot off at ground level with a knife or scissors. The flowers are the next edible part to harvest in early summer. They make good vegetables when they are unopened buds, just pluck them off the flower stalk when they are still green and firm. The opened, orange flower petals and sepals can be collected in the morning when they are still firm. At the end of the day, the wilted flower parts can be collected and dried further or used lightly wilted in recipes. The tubers are best dug in fall or early spring before the plant starts sending out shoots. This way, more of the plant's energy is stored in the tubers for overwintering, and the tubers are plump. If you try to dig up the tubers in the wrong season, they will appear deflated and won't be worth your time to prep and cook. You can find the tubers by observing a colony of daylilies during its active growth periods and returning to that place in fall or spring when there are no leaves. Digging with a large pitchfork is easiest, but a shovel will work as well. Try not to remove more than 25 percent of the tuber clumps to allow the colony to thrive.

Eating and Preserving

The daylily shoots have a mild oniony flavor to them, and are nice and crunchy when picked fresh. They can be nibbled raw or added to stir fries. The unopened flower buds need to be lightly sautéed in oil or boiled before eating; we have used them in place of a portion of elbow macaroni in baked mac and cheese. The opened, orange flower parts can be batter-dipped and fried or chopped raw into salads for a colorful and mildly onion-like flavor. You may have already eaten the wilted flowers in traditional Chinese Hot and Sour soup or Moo Shu Pork dishes, where they are referred to as "golden needles". We used to buy them at the Asian market in bags already dried, but now we can gather our own, dehydrate them, and store them in airtight jars. The dried flower parts can be reconstituted and added to recipes, or added to soups for their thickening qualities. The flower buds and petals are good sources of beta carotene and vitamin C. When dug at the right time, the tubers look like a bunch of fingerling potatoes, and can be used in many similar ways. We think they have a slightly sweet flavor, so we shredded them and used them to make a cake, but they can be scrubbed (peeling is not mandatory if you scrub them well), boiled and mashed, or sliced and fried for a nutty and starchy wild food. *Note*: Daylily is one wild food that is wise to try in small amounts to see how your body reacts. A small percentage of people will experience gastrointestinal upset when they consume large amounts of daylily.

Linden Flowers, Lime Tree, Basswood N

Tilia americana

The flowers of the linden tree make a favorite herbal tisane and syrup in our house. The intensely fragrant flowers are easy to gather and dry in large quantities to use as a relaxing warm drink during cold New England winters; it is soothing to the throat and mildly sedative, a perfect tonic for cold season.

The flowers and light green bracts of the linden tree

How to Identify

Lindens can reach a height of eighty feet and have greyish-brown bark with vertical fissures along the trunk of the tree. The leaves are alternately arranged, egg- shaped and wider at the asymmetrical base, 3 to 5 inches wide, coarsely toothed, and shiny green when mature. The twigs and leaves contain a mucilaginous sap. The flowers are very fragrant and grow in short racemes of 6 to 20 flowers attached to a light green, elongated leaf bract that stands out from the darker green leaves. The flowers are yellowish-white and have 5 petals, 5 sepals, and numerous stamens. The flowers will become small, fuzzy, cream colored round nutlets in late summer.

Habitat and Range

The American linden is native to North America and grows east of the Rockies up through eastern Canada. It will grow in mixed forests, but prefers soil with a high pH. Lindens are attractive trees often planted in landscaped areas and parking lots. Harvesting the young leaves in spring or gathering the aromatic flowers will not harm the tree since you couldn't possibly reach the highest branches of the tree. They spread through underground suckers and even cut trees will sprout new growth from the stumps.

Robert is using his hands-free basket tied to his waist to collect
the linden flowers from low branches

When and How to Harvest

In the spring when the new leaves are unfurling and still a bit downy, they can be collected as a spring green. We gather the flowers once they start opening in late spring. This is a great use for a hands-free picking container, as you can gently bend a branch down with one hand and pluck the entire light green leaf bract attached to the flowers right off and drop it into the basket. You'll get sticky hands from the sweet nectar, and might have to shake quite a few bees and beetles from the flowers, but collecting large amounts of the flowers can be easy from smaller trees.

Eating and Preserving

When the very young leaves are tender and still lightly translucent they make good additions to raw salads and can be used to thicken soups because of their mucilaginous qualities. The fresh flowers and bracts make a light yellow, perfumed syrup for sodas and cocktails. We dry the flowers loosely packed in large paper bags kept in a dark place for a week or so, shaking the contents every day to evenly distribute them. After they are dry, keep them in airtight containers to use all year for a medicinal infusion and refreshing brewed drink. The flowers and bracts contain volatile oils, flavonoids which act as antioxidants, and the mucilaginous constituents reduce inflammation and soothe sore throats. The infusion is sweet enough that even kids will enjoy sipping it. We love to infuse syrups with fragrant flowers, and then use the syrups as a base for homemade sodas. This basic syrup recipe can be used for any aromatic flowers using clean, fresh flowers.

Linden Flower Syrup

Makes about 4 cups of syrup

2 ¼ cups water
3 cups sugar

2 cups packed linden flowers and leaf bracts
3 Tablespoons ascorbic acid powder (vitamin C)

1. Heat the water to boiling and add the sugar. Remove from the heat, and stir until the sugar dissolves.
2. Allow the sugar syrup to cool to 80°F, then add the linden flowers and leaf bracts. Let the flowers steep in the syrup for 24 hours.
3. Filter out the flowers and give them a squeeze to extract all of their flavor.
4. Remove 1 cup of the syrup, and warm it up. Add the ascorbic acid, stirring to dissolve. Pour the syrup back into the rest, mixing well. Store the syrup in airtight glass jars or bottles. To make a sweet and fragrant drink, add 3 Tablespoons of the syrup to 12 oz. plain seltzer water and stir.

Pineapple Weed I

Matricaria discoidea
Resembling its botanical cousin, chamomile, pineapple weed is a common non-native weed that can be used to make a pineapple-scented herbal tisane.

Pineapple weed flowers appear to not have petals

How to Identify

Pineapple weed is a short herbaceous weed between 2 to 15 inches tall with alternate, finely divided leaves that appear feathery. The composite flower heads are yellowish-green, cone shaped, and appear to not have any petals, but are actually many small, densely packed tubular flowers that form the cone shaped head. All parts of the plant have a pineapple scent when crushed.

Habitat and Range

Pineapple weed grows in disturbed areas with poor, compact soil. It can be found growing in full sun along paths, in driveways, fields and at roadsides. We gather large quantities at the edge of the gravely roads at the organic farm from which we get our vegetables in the summer. Originally from northern Asia and the Russian Far East, it has become naturalized throughout all of North America. Pineapple weed can be gathered in large quantities without harming the population; it also bounces back quickly even when mowed repeatedly.

When and How to Harvest

We start collecting the flower heads and feathery foliage in mid-summer through the fall. All parts can be collected with scissors, or break off the above ground parts with your fingers. Leave a bit of leaves and the root intact to insure future harvests from the same spot.

Eating and Preserving

We dry the flower heads to use later in the winter, but a nicely flavored infusion can be made from fresh or dried parts of the plant. Use about one tablespoon of leaves and flowers to one cup of hot water; allow it to infuse while covered for about 15 minutes, then filter out the solids. Sweeten and enjoy, or chill the infusion for a nice iced drink. Kids will enjoy the flavor of pineapple weed infusion, and will even like to nibble the raw flower heads. I have often found a forgotten handful of flower heads in Gillian's pockets that she collected for herself while we are out foraging.

Red Clover I

Trifolium pratense

The state flower of Vermont and national flower of Denmark, red clover flowers are sweet trail nibbles for kids and make delightful herbal tisanes for the whole family.

Red clover flowers with their easily recognizable leaves

How to Identify

Red clovers are perennial herbs with alternate and trifoliate leaves; each leaf has three elongated oval leaflets with a paler chevron mark on the upper surface. They are variable in height, growing 8 to 20 inches tall, but often sprawling along the ground. The leaflets and stalks are lightly hairy. The flowers look like pink or purplish-red pom-poms about an inch in diameter. The flower head is made up of many smaller florets attached to a core.

Habitat and Range

Red clover grows in sunny areas along roadsides, in lawns, and is often planted as a cover crop for farm fields as red clover fixes nitrogen into the soil for future crops. Initially introduced from Europe, red clover has become naturalized throughout all of North America. Harvesting the flower head will not impact the population as red clover regrows from its roots every year.

When and How to Harvest

While the leaves can be eaten after cooking, we don't bother with them. We collect the flower heads by popping them off the stalks into collecting baskets and buckets as soon as they start blooming in mid-spring through the summer; mowing fields of red clover will encourage it to produce flowers in succession over a longer period. Collect only the flowers that are fully pink or purplish-red, avoid the flower heads that have traces of brown or have wilted.

Eating and Preserving

The flowers of the red clover are ideal morsels for kids to snack on. Gently pluck each floret from the bristly core and suck on the end to get a little burst of nectar, then eat the pink flower for a sweet treat. The plucked florets can be added to salads for a little color and sweetness. We dry the intact flower heads in a paper bag in a dark room for a week or so, then store the dried, light pink flower heads in an airtight jar. Make a floral infusion from the dried flower heads in hot water, covered and steeped for 15-20 minutes and lightly sweetened with honey (you can even buy clover honey to sweeten your clover infusion!) to soothe coughs and as an expectorant.

Violets I, N

Viola species

Abundant, pretty, and mild in flavor, wild violets make nice additions to wild green salads and in sweet desserts.

Beautiful violets

How to Identify

Wild violets have heart-shaped, lightly scalloped leaves growing from a basal rosette on short stems. When the leaves first emerge in early spring, they are furled up like a scroll. The flowers grow from a leafless stalk and have five petals; with two top petals, two ornamented side petals, and a fifth lowest petal that is often elongated and deeply veined. The pretty flower roughly resembles a butterfly. Violets are various shades of blue, purple, white and occasionally yellow. Not all cultivated violets and pansies are edible, and African violets are not botanically related to wild violets.

Habitat and Range

Wild violets can pop up in yards and gardens, but prefer moist woodlands where they get dappled sunlight. There are many species of violets in North America, some native and some introduced invasives; violets will readily interbreed and hybridize so identifying violets to species can be difficult. Harvesting tender leaves of violets in spring and the showy flowers will not harm the plant as it spreads through roots and prolific seed production.

When and How to Harvest

The leaves can be harvested in early spring when they first emerge looking like rolled up scrolls. Snip the short stems with scissors or snap them off with your hands. The flowers bloom in spring and may persist through the summer in cooler areas. A second flush of blooms may be seen in the late fall, right before it frosts, and these late flowers produce the seed pods. Pluck them off their short stems and use immediately or store in the refrigerator for a short period.

Brilliantly colored and lightly fragrant violet jelly

Eating and Preserving

The young leaves have a gummy, mucilaginous quality, but they can be eaten raw in salads, lightly cooked as mild greens or added to soups. The flowers of many of the violets that grow in the Northeast have very little fragrance; we collect them for their beauty and whimsy. We add them to salads, freeze them in ice cubes for garnish, and candy them for edible sweet decorations. In the past, I have made brilliantly colored jellies from an infusion of the flowers, but the flavor was too delicate to taste much besides the sugar. The English violet is highly perfumed and makes a more flavorful jelly and flower syrup and may be worth growing in your garden.

CHAPTER 8:

Foraging Leaves, Greens, Shoots, Stems, Stalks, and Twigs

You may be wondering how many salads we will suggest you eat made with the wild greens included in this chapter, because what else could you possibly do with green and leaves? Many of the slightly bitter greens or tender leaves make excellent cooking greens; much more nutritious than their store-bought cousins, and free for anyone willing to seek them out. Some wild greens and leaves are gourmet food items, highly sought by professional chefs. The shoots and stalks are the young, tender parts of growing plants, if collected at the correct time in the plant's life cycle, make fantastic foods of early spring filled with new life and energy; many of these tender greens will come back in the cooler autumn months as well, providing a second burst of fresh nutrition. The majority of leaves, greens, and shoots are surprisingly cosmopolitan and will grow anywhere including your home garden or yard, making it easy to gather them for meals. Some of the tender greens and leaves are seasonal, and can be collected, lightly blanched, and frozen to use in other seasons for nutritional, local food all year. And yes, you will be able to add the raw leaves and greens to a wild food salad, along with wild flowers for a pop of foraged color and taste.

The non-tender leaves and sticks can be used as wild flavorings or in ways similar to spices to enhance your cooking. We like to identify several of them by the scratch-and-sniff method, where you scratch a portion of the bark or skin of the stem to get a strong and distinct fragrance. Kids will get pretty excited by the idea of some familiar smells being found in nature, and will be enchanted by some new, almost exotic smells they can find in their own neighborhood.

Sampling the greens, leaves, and stalks in this chapter may introduce you to new flavors, like bitter, pungent, or sour. While children will readily eat things that are sour, it may take a few tries to get them to eat the stronger flavored wild foods. Less agreeable flavors like bitter or pungent have largely been hybridized and bred out of the common foods you find at the grocery store to appeal to broader tastes, so even adults might have to give them more than one try before making a final judgment. The high nutritional values, local availability, novelty, and non-existent costs of wild greens, leaves, stalks and shoots should be great motivators to broaden your palate and give you plenty of incentive to make them a large part of your potential wild foraged diet.

A few simple tips can be used to get the most out of safely and successfully foraging for wild greens, leaves, shoots, and twigs.

- ✓ Know the seasonality or correct time to harvest greens and leaves; it can make a large difference in their edibility, texture, and flavor. Get to know the plant or shrub even when it is not is season so you can recognize and remember new locations for potential foraging at the right times.
- ✓ Taste new greens, leaves, and stalks more than once to give yourself a chance to experience their new flavors; sometimes just combining them with more familiar or bland greens is better than not eating them at all and you can still get some of their benefits.
- ✓ Know your foraging environment and avoid pesticides, fertilizers, and other chemicals, and avoid areas that animals use to relieve themselves. For many of these plants, your foraging location can be your own yard or garden.

Collecting the greens, leaves and other parts of plants or shrubs is easily accomplished with a knife, scissors for the kids, or a small set of pruners. You won't be taking the whole plant, so it's a non-lethal collection for the plant if a small portion of the leaves are harvested at a time. Many of the greens and leaves are from plants that are prolific seeders, and some can be very invasive, crowding out the native population of plants, so collecting in large quantities for preservation like freezing or pickling is encouraged.

The leaves, greens, stems, or shoots of these other wild plants are edible, but are discussed in more detail in other sections of this book because of additional, more useful parts:

- Burdock
- Daylily
- Grapes

- Linden
- Wintergreen
- Violets

Bamboo Shoots I

Phyllostachys aureosulcata

An incredibly invasive plant, bamboo is often mistakenly landscaped in yards with destructive consequences, but we can still collect and eat the shoots without further spreading a patch.

Robert peels the outer leaves off of yellow groove bamboo
shoots to get to the tender hearts

How to Identify

Bamboo is botanically a grass. The hollow, chambered main stalks can grow up to 23-30 feet tall, and have alternate branches on the main stalk, with a distinctive yellow groove on the stalk that alternates with the branches. The leaves are 1-4 inches long, thin and pointed, and in our cooler climate they are deciduous; in warmer climates they persist all year. The shoots are initially covered with a papery sheath that can have stripes of purple, yellow, and green, but this sheath falls away as the branches grow and expand. The hollow stalks darken from light green to dark green with age, and have a rough outer surface.

Habitat and Range

Yellow groove bamboo grows in subtropical climates through temperate climates, and is cold tolerant. It is originally from eastern Asia, but has become a common invasive that spreads aggressively through underground rhizomes. It grows in lawns, along waterways, and in waste areas. Never plant yellow groove bamboo intentionally, as it is difficult to eradicate. Collecting the shoots will not harm a patch of bamboo.

When and How to Harvest

The shoots of yellow groove bamboo can be collected for about three weeks in mid-spring. We collect the shoots that are about 1-3 feet tall and still covered in the striped sheath. Once they get too much taller, the interior crosswalls of the stalk toughen too much to eat. Use a knife to collect the top 12-16 inches of the shoot, it should slice off easily.

Soba noodles with foraged bamboo shoots

Eating and Preserving

Bamboo shoots are mostly water, and are a low-calorie, high-fiber vegetable popular in Asia. They can be eaten raw, boiled, pickled, canned, roasted and grilled. Not all species of bamboo are edible, some are rather bitter and others may contain a cyanogenic glycoside, (taxiphyllin), which can change to hydrogen cyanide in your gut. This toxin breaks down in water, so just to be safe, we boil our bamboo shoots. We then slice the shoot lengthwise first before sliding a thumb between the chambered shoot and the sheath; the leafy sheath should come away from the stalk quite easily. We then boil the split shoots for about 15-20 minutes in water with added rice or rice bran, which is the traditional Japanese way to prepare *takenoko*. The shoots are then drained and can be tossed with some soy sauce and ginger, or lemon juice and olive oil. They make a fantastic cold salad or noodle dish addition, or delicious stir-fry vegetable. The boiled shoots can be frozen for later use.

Bayberry Leaves N

Morella pensylvanica, Morella caroliniensis
Found in eastern North America and along southern coasts, bayberry leaves can be used as an aromatic seasoning, and the berries can be used to make traditional, scented candles.

Leaves and berries from a northern, female bay laurel shrub

How to Identify

Bayberry bushes grow up to ten feet tall, but are often stunted when found on coastal beaches, and it is a common and attractive landscaping plant. The branches are grey and brittle, and its leaves are alternate and elongated, 1-3 inches long, toothed at the ends, leathery, and emit a pleasant, spicy odor when crushed. The small flower catkins grow directly from the branches and range from green to red in color. The waxy berries only appear on the female bushes if male bushes are nearby to pollinate the flowers, and are wrinkly, blue-grey, and hard.

Habitat and Range

Northern bayberry (*Morella pensylvanica*) is a deciduous shrub growing in eastern North America from Newfoundland west to Ontario and Ohio, and south to North Carolina. The southern bayberry (*Morella caroliniensis*) is evergreen and ranges from Maryland to Texas. They will grow along beaches, and in inland areas such as open fields and along edges of woodlands, preferring full sun or partial shade. Bayberry can tolerate poor soil because they have nitrogen fixing capabilities due to a symbiotic relationship with bacteria. Both bayberry species are native to North America. Removing some of the leaves or collecting the berries will not harm the bayberry shrub as they spread readily in colonies through their roots.

When and How to Harvest

The leaves can be harvested at any time in the summer and autumn. Gently pluck a few leaves from each branch into a paper bag, and dry in a dark, dry place. We sometimes press them flat in pages of books and they end up less brittle. The berries can be collected into buckets or hands-free collecting containers in mid-summer through late fall when they are coated with the blue-grey wax.

Eating and Preserving

The leaves of bayberry have a similar flavor to commercial Mediterranean bay leaves, and can be used in the same way to flavor soups. Bayberry is milder in flavor, so we add a few more than a recipe calls for and remove them from the soup before eating since the leaves themselves are not edible. An easy method for their later removal is to place them in a large tea ball or a cheesecloth satchel, rather than fishing them out with a spoon. They keep for long periods in airtight jars once dried. The berries can be used to make perfumed candles.

Bayberry Candles

Bayberry candles were made by the colonists to use as a fragrant replacement for the often rancid tallow candles they burned. Folklore states that if you light a new bayberry candle on Christmas Eve and allow it to burn into the next morning, you'll have health, wealth and prosperity in the coming year. The adage reads: "A bayberry candle burnt to the socket brings food to the larder and gold to the pocket". We have experimented with mixed success with candle making with the northern bayberries in our area; using the southern bayberries will yield more wax per gallon of collected berries.

Bayberry candles and some of the wax-laden berries

Starting with one gallon of waxy berries, gently shake them in a mesh sieve to remove some of the small debris. Place the berries in a large pot with water and lightly simmer the berries for about 15 minutes. The berries, stems, and most of the twigs will sink to the bottom of the pot, while the wax will float to the top. Try not to simmer them too vigorously or some of the fragrant oils will evaporate. The hot wax along with some of the hot water is ladled out and strained through an old mesh jelly bag (cheese cloth will work as well) into a plastic container to get out the finer debris particles. Once the water and wax cool, remove the hardened wax block from the container and dry it off with a towel, yielding about ⅓ of a cup of fragrant, green wax.

To stretch the small amount of bayberry wax and create a stronger and cleaner-burning candle, add a bit of paraffin or beeswax from the craft store and re-melt them together before pouring the wax into votive molds with wicks. A few hours later, the candles will have hardened and can be unmolded, beautiful and aromatic, ready to be burned on Christmas Eve.

Birch Trees N

Betula alleghaniensis, Betula lenta
Twigs and inner bark of birches can be used as flavorings for teas and birch beer, and larger trees can be tapped for sap to make your own syrup. Kids will like to use the scratch-and-sniff method to help identify birch twigs.

Bark of black birch showing the horizontal lenticels,
and leaf stems of black birch

How to Identify

Yellow birch (*Betula alleghaniensis*) is a medium sized deciduous tree with smooth, yellow bark that flakes off in horizontal strips. Black, or sweet birch (*Betula lenta*) is a medium sized deciduous tree with smooth, silvery-grey bark that does not peel but has horizontal light grey lenticels. Both species of trees have alternate, ovate, finely toothed leaves, male catkins that are 1-2 inches long that are pendulous, and female catkins that are ½-1 inch long that stand upright. The female catkins bear the small, winged seeds that mature in fall when the leaves of birches turn a pretty golden-yellow. Peeling the twigs or scratching the bark will reveal an important identifying characteristic: the inner cambium layer smells strongly of wintergreen.

Habitat and Range

Birch trees are native, pioneer trees and will often be the first saplings to grow in abandoned fields, disturbed areas, or after fires. They grow in mixed upland forests and near water, and are common in the eastern half of North America from Ontario down to the upper elevations of Georgia. Collecting some twigs will not harm the trees, but collecting sap or the inner bark should be done with care. Trees for tapping should be larger than 20 inches in diameter, and the inner bark is best collected from recently cut or broken trees to prevent rot or insect infestations from killing live trees.

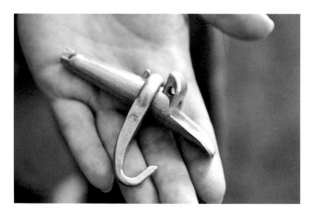

A spile like this is used to tap trees for collecting sap

When and How to Harvest

The twigs of birch can be gathered all year to chew or make into tea. The inner bark can also be collected all year, but it is best to find freshly cut trees or broken limbs to remove the cambium. Birch sap runs a few weeks after maple sap has finished, when you see the leaf buds beginning to swell, in mid-March through early April. We tap the trees using a drill and a spile, and retrieve the 5-gallon buckets of sap twice a day until the sap begins to run cloudy.

Eating and Preserving

The volatile oil in the twigs and outer bark that give birch its wintergreen flavor is methyl salicylate. It has mild pain relieving, anti-inflammatory, and fever reducing properties. We chew on the peeled fresh twigs to relieve mild gum pain; Gillian loves the flavor and is often seen hiking with a twig in her mouth. The twigs and inner cambium layer can be collected and used to make a cold infusion in water to preserve the volatile oils that would otherwise dissipate in a boiled water infusion; steep the twigs or bark, covered, in room temperature water for 2-4 hours. The inner bark can be dried, but twigs are best picked and used fresh. We drink the sap of the birch raw in the early spring for a clean, refreshing spring tonic that contains natural fructose and glucose in small amounts; the sugar content of birch is much lower than maple, so you would need 100 quarts of sap to produce one quart of syrup! The sap should be reduced over a fire or a burner outdoors because of the excessive condensation that would occur on your kitchen walls. The syrup of birch will have a molasses-like flavor and be thinner than traditional syrup, but contains vitamin C, manganese, and calcium. Store any syrup in the refrigerator.

Chickweed I

Stellaria media
Chickweed is likely one of the plants that you are probably weeding *out* of your garden. Tender and tasty, chickweed is easily incorporated

Chickweed flowers, leaves, and the stem showing the
"mohawk" of hair down one side

into meals, salads, or green smoothies, and one the kids will defi-
nitely eat.

How to Identify

Chickweed is a low-growing herbaceous annual plant with small,
opposite leaves growing in pairs from nodes at the end of each seg-
ment of the stem. Each stem can grow up to a sprawling 18 inches
long, or the plant can grow in more compact, upright bunches. The
leaves are oval with pointy tips, have smooth edges, short stems, and
are ½-1 inch long. The stems have a single line of hair running down
their length, like a miniature mohawk hairstyle, switching position on
the stem between the nodes on the stem. There is a tough, white string
in the core of the stem that can be observed by pinching the stem
partially open and gently pulling it apart; the core acts like a rubber

band to keep the stem together. The flowers are small and white with 5 deeply split petals that appear as 10 petals at first glance, and have 5 sepals with hairy undersides beneath the petals. Use a magnifier to observe the split flower petals and the hairs on the stem.

Habitat and Range

Chickweed is an invasive and now naturalized plant from Europe, found throughout all of North America. It will grow in gardens, disturbed soil, abandoned lots, in parks, farmland, and along the foundation of your house. Chickweed prefers partial shade and will get tough in full sun. Cutting the tops of the stems will help the plant produce lush new growth, and no matter how often you pull it as a weed it will grow right back, so overharvest isn't a problem.

When and How to Harvest

Chickweed is a tender, cool weather plant, growing in spring and seeding itself for a second crop in the fall. You can even find patches of fresh chickweed during a mild winter or in protected areas under light snow. In the heat of summer, they die back completely or sprawl out and get stringy. It is generally the top two inches of the stem that are the most tender and the best edible part. This will include the flower buds and flowers, which are equally tender, mild, and edible. Harvesting from a thick bunch is easiest using a pair of scissors to snip off the tops, then wash and spin them dry in a salad spinner. Don't try to eat any more than the top 2 inches of the stems; otherwise eating the stems will be like eating straw. All of the leaves will remain tender, and can be stripped off the entire stem, but it is easiest to consume the stem tops, leaves, and flowers all together.

Eating and Preserving

Chickweed is tender and mild, with a slight corn-silk flavor. We use it as a green garnish for things we cook and eat in the spring when we are starved for fresh seasonal greens, or use it like sprouts in recipes.

Chickweed is an obvious addition to salads and a great mild green that can be mixed with stronger greens when cooking, although you won't want to cook chickweed very long, 3-5 minutes at most. Gillian loves chickweed; she can identify it easily, it tastes good, and she picks it on her own to snack on. Because of its tender nature, we don't bother to preserve or save chickweed for later use. It is so abundant in the spring and again in the fall, we pick and eat it immediately.

Dandelion I ☆

Taraxacum officinale

With edible leaves, flowers, and roots, the dandelion is a plant that is in need of an image makeover from evil lawn weed to culinary and nutritional sensation. Let the kids blow the fluffy seed heads, planting wild food as they play, or use the hollow flower stems as whimsical, natural drinking straws.

A very healthy basal rosette with many flower stalks can grow from a single taproot

How to Identify

Dandelions are herbaceous perennial plants that grow from basal rosettes attached to a long taproot. The leaves can vary in length and appearances based on growing conditions, but are generally 2-16 inches long and ½-3 inches wide, and lance shaped with lobed or toothed edges. Each taproot can produce multiple unbranched flower stalks that are hollow, sometimes tinged with purple, sparsely covered with small hairs, and have a single flower head. The leaves and flower stem will exude milky latex when cut. The familiar yellow flower is actually composed of many small ray florets that look like petals, and can be up to 1½ inches wide. The white pom-pom seed heads form after the flower matures, with silky tufts that make them easily dispersed by the wind or kids who blow them to make wishes. The taproot has light brown skin on the outside and is greyish-white inside, is brittle, and up to 24 inches long.

Habitat and Range

Dandelions thrive in disturbed habitats, sunny fields, lawns, along hiking paths, in gardens, and on farms. Dandelions were originally from Europe and Asia, but have been naturalized throughout all temperate regions of the globe, including all of North America. Collecting them will not affect their population since they are prolific seeders.

When and How to Harvest

The leaves are best harvested from younger plants in the spring before they flower by cutting the central leaves from the basal rosette with scissors. As the summer progresses and the plant spends more time in the sun, the leaves become more bitter. Root crowns are referred to as "lawn squid" when they emerge in the spring; they are the white and purple-tinged, bulging bases of the leaves that are attached to the taproot. The unopened and opened flower heads can be collected in the in late spring and summer mornings, plucked from the stem before it wilts in the evening. They pop off the tall, hollow stem easily. The taproot is best dug in the fall or spring after it rains with a small gardening trowel, trying to get as much of the root before it breaks off.

Dandelion root showing the purple root crowns called lawn squid

Eating and Preserving

As a cooked green, dandelion can provide more iron and calcium than cultivated spinach, as well as vitamins A, B, C, and E. When gathered in the spring, the leaves are only mildly bitter and can be mixed with blander greens in recipes. The chopped leaves should be boiled for 4-10 minutes or lightly sautéed to alleviate the potential bitterness, and then added to baked dishes; anything with cheese and eggs works well with the flavor of dandelion greens. If the leaves are young enough, they can be eaten raw in mixed salads in small amounts, chopped into bite-sized pieces. This is one plant I urge you to try several times to become accustomed to the slight bitter flavor. The quality of the greens varies with age, location, and growing conditions, and often the bitterness can be managed and reduced with boiling in clean water. The root crowns can be used roasted or boiled as a cooked vegetable in stews and casseroles. Tightly closed flower buds can be used to make pickles, or boiled and added to stir fries with other vegetables. The yellow flower heads and individual florets make beautiful, edible garnishes for salads and other dishes; Gillian will pluck them and chew the yellow parts from the bitter green calyx while we are out walking, sometimes leaving a patch of yellow pollen on her nose. We also use the yellow florets to make a dandelion jelly and wine; pinch off the green calyx and most of the yellow florets will fall free. Robert enjoys using the taproots to make a caffeine-free coffee substitute by digging, scrubbing, and chopping the taproots, then roasting them in the oven until brown and hard. He then grinds them in a coffee grinder and filters boiling water through the powder. The smell is similar to dark chocolate, with a bitter coffee taste, much improved with some sugar and milk.

Dandelion Jelly
Makes About 5-8 Oz. Jars

4 cups dandelion flower petals, green bits removed
4 cups water

1. Place the dandelion flower petals in a pot and add the water, bring to a boil and reduce to a simmer. Simmer 10 minutes, then turn off heat and allow the pot to cool.

2. Use a jelly bag or coffee filter to strain the flowers out of the water, you need 3 cups of dandelion infusion to make the jelly, but may have some extra.

 3 cups dandelion infusion
 1 Tablespoon lemon juice
 1 box Sure-Jell powdered pectin
 4 ½ cups sugar

3. Place dandelion infusion, lemon juice, and pectin powder in a large pot. Whisk together and bring this mixture to a rolling boil.

4. Add all of the sugar at once, stirring constantly, and return the mixture to a rolling boil. Boil 2 minutes.

5. Remove the jelly from the heat, skim the foam from the top and ladle into sterilized hot jars. Cover, and process in a water bath for 10 minutes.

Garlic Mustard I ☆

Alliaria petiolata

An invasive plant that naturalists love to hate, wild food foragers can help control garlic mustard by eating it. We field many requests from conservation groups to use our recipes in pamphlets encouraging the consumption of this weed in efforts to curb its spread. Knowing when to use different parts of this fully edible plant can be your key to enjoying garlic mustard in all of its growth stages and seasons.

How to Identify

Garlic mustard is a biennial herbaceous plant, producing flowers and seeds in its second year. In its first season, garlic mustard grows in a

Second year flower stalks and first year basal rosettes of garlic mustard

basal rosette from a white taproot; the leaves are kidney-shaped with scalloped edges, 1-4 inches wide, long stems, and can either overwinter in milder climates or lose its leaves in colder climates. In the second season of growth, the flower stalks appear in early spring with alternate sets of triangular to heart-shaped leaves with toothed edges. The branched flower stalk can grow more than 3 feet tall in ideal conditions and produces white, four petaled flowers in broccoli-like clusters at the tips of the stems, which soon develop into 1-3 inch, elongated green seed pods called siliques. As the seeds mature, the pods will dry up and turn brown before splitting open to disperse the small, 1/8 inch long black seeds. Some of the seeds that were dropped in the summer will start sprouting in the fall, so you'll see the basal leaves again. All herbaceous parts of the plant emit a strong garlic smell when crushed, and the seeds and roots have a horseradish-like bite.

Habitat and Range

Garlic mustard prefers partially shaded areas and disturbed soils in fields and yard edges. Originally from Europe and Asia, it has become a noxious pest in central and eastern North America, and the Pacific Northwest through Alaska. Garlic mustard is a successful invader for several reasons; it seeds prolifically, its biennial nature allows it to sprout and grow before the native trees leaf out and block the sun, and it has no natural enemies in North America to keep it in check. Garlic mustard also employs phytochemicals that effect mycorrhiza of fungi and inhibits native plants from germinating, creating entire colonies of garlic mustard that continue to spread further each season. Collecting garlic mustard for consumption or removing garlic mustard for ecological reasons will not harm this invader.

When and How to Harvest

All of the leaves of garlic mustard are edible, but can vary in toughness. If you have a spot where you know there is an abundance of garlic mustard, you can collect the tiny cotyledons that emerge in early spring in large quantities to use like spicy sprouts. The basal leaves can be cut off with scissors in the spring or fall before they toughen. The flower stalks can be snapped off about 3-4 inches from the top before the stalk becomes fibrous in late spring. The flower clusters are tender and edible after a 3 minute boil, and the small flowers are edible raw. The seed pods are edible while still light green, and seeds can be used once they have dried and turned black in early summer. Gather the seeds by collecting the entire dried, brown seed pod in a bucket and then crushing them, splitting the pods open. The heavier seeds will fall to the bottom of your container, and the pods can be winnowed away by gently blowing on the chaff. The spicy taproot can be dug before the plant flowers; it is often small and stringy, but enough can be easily collected from a dense stand of garlic mustard.

Eating and Preserving

While the first year's basal leaves are edible as greens, we prefer to collect and eat the triangular leaves from the second year's flower stalk due to texture; the basal leaves are a bit tougher while the flower

The clustered flower head with a few white blossoms, the stalk showing the triangular, toothed leaves, and the same stalk showing the siliques, or seed pods, holding the small black seeds

stalk leaves are more tender. Sometimes the leaves of garlic mustard are lush and so large that they can be used like wraps for small sandwiches or grain-filled pouches. The leaves benefit from a bit of cooking, and they retain their garlicky-mustard flavor even after boiling or sautéing. We parboil the leaves and chop them roughly, then flat-pack them into freezer bags to use all year in multiple recipes. Many people make a pungent pesto with garlic mustard leaves, which also freezes well for future use. If you find garlic mustard a little bitter, try it again in the early spring and look for younger growth, or boil it for a longer period to alleviate some bitterness. When the flower stalks have unopened flower clusters in their tops, we snap off about 3-4 inches of the top and boil it to eat like a zesty broccoli floret with a little butter and salt. The pretty, white flowers can be added raw to salads or sandwiches for a spicy kick. The young, green seed pods can be collected and nibbled raw or boiled briefly and eaten like a vegetable. For us, the mature seeds are the best part of garlic mustard; the more we can eat, the less garlic mustard plants can sprout later. We add them to breads, toast them to add to curries, and we grind them for a sinus-clearing spicy mustard used on sandwiches and in dressings. Once collected and dried further, the seeds can be stored in a sealed container or the freezer. If you dig a large quantity of roots, they can be cleaned then pulverized in the food processor with a bit of vinegar for a wild, homemade horseradish-like condiment. Garlic mustard is high in fiber, beta-carotene, vitamin C and E, and zinc, plus calcium, iron, omega-3 fatty acids, and manganese. With so many useful parts, great taste, and its high nutritional content, it amazes me that more people don't harvest garlic mustard as a free, wild edible.

Garlic Mustard Roulade

Makes one 12" roll, about 8 servings

1 pound garlic mustard greens, stems removed
½ teaspoon ground nutmeg
½ teaspoon sea salt
1 teaspoon smoked paprika
2 teaspoon granulated garlic
½ teaspoon ground black pepper

4 egg yolks
4 egg whites
2cups shredded mozzarella cheese or filling of your choice

1. Heat oven to 425° F. Prepare a sheet pan with a parchment paper liner.

2. In a large pot of boiling water, blanch the garlic mustard greens for 1 minute. Shock the greens in ice water to stop the cooking process, and squeeze as much water from them as possible.

3. Add the cooked greens to a food processor. Add the nutmeg, salt, smoked paprika, granulated garlic, black pepper and egg yolks. Pulse until the garlic mustard greens are finely chopped.

4. In a mixer, whip the egg whites until stiff peaks form. With a spatula, fold ⅓ of the egg whites into the greens mixture, mixing until no more whites are seen. Then gently fold in the remaining egg whites, until the mixture is uniform.

5. Spread the garlic mustard and egg mixture evenly on the parchment paper covered sheet pan, leaving an inch of exposed paper around the entire edge. Bake until the egg is set, about 12-15 minutes.

6. Loosen the roulade from the parchment paper. Sprinkle the top with whatever you are using as a filling, or just shredded cheese.

7. Starting with the wider side, roll the roulade up like a jelly roll, ending seam side down. Bake an additional 10 minutes to melt the cheese and warm the filling.

The abundant seeds of garlic mustard can be made into a spicy mustard

Garlic Mustard-Mustard

Makes about ½ cup

7 Tablespoons ground garlic mustard seeds (use an electric coffee grinder)
2 teaspoons apple cider vinegar
½ teaspoon salt
6 Tablespoons water
2 teaspoon agave syrup or honey
¼ teaspoon turmeric

1. Whisk together the ground seeds with the salt and turmeric. Whisk in the water, honey and vinegar until smooth.

2. Allow the mustard to sit for a week in the refrigerator. It will need to be stirred before use and the color will darken. Keep stored, covered, in the fridge for up to a year.

Hairy Bittercress I

Cardamine hirsute

Often overlooked because of its diminutive size, hairy bittercress is one of the earliest spring greens that we forage. Packing a peppery punch, it adds zing to salads and is a thrill for children when it flings its seeds when touched in a mini explosion, giving it its other common name, shotweed.

Hairy bittercress basal rosette with its flower stalk and small white flowers

How to Identify

Hairy bittercress is an annual herbaceous plant in the mustard family. It forms a basal rosette with each leaf bearing 5-9 circular leaflets on a 2-4 inch stringy stem that has a few long hairs and is dull purple.

The leaflets on the outer edge of the rosette are larger than the inner leaflets, and the terminal leaflet is much larger than the side leaflets. A single flower stalk grows up to 10 inches tall from the center of the rosette, bearing small, white, four-petaled flowers that develop into elongated seed pods called siliques. The roots are shallow and stringy, and the leaves have a pungent taste.

Habitat and Range

Originally from Europe and Asia, hairy bittercress is an invasive weed that is found along both coasts of North America, and through the central and southern United States. It grows in poor soil along margins of paths, at roadsides, in old fields, and disturbed soils. Collecting hairy bittercress is not a concern since it prolifically spreads its seeds with force when the ripe seed pods are touched.

When and How to Harvest

When the snow has finally melted and the days are warming, we are craving some fresh greens in the early spring months of March and April. Hairy bittercress is a low-lying plant, often stepped on and overlooked. We go to old fields to harvest the whole rosettes in bags, just pulling them out of the dirt with our fingers, and then wash them in a big bowl of cold water before spinning them dry in the salad spinner and separating the leaves from the rosettes to use. Hairy bittercress self-seeds and may sprout again in the cooler autumn months.

Eating and Preserving

We eat several mixed salads with hairy bittercress in the early spring season. They can be added raw to grain salads as well as green salads. Their taste is similar to watercress, and their peppery bite makes a nice, creamy dressing or dip. We use them fresh and seasonally, eagerly anticipating their return each spring.

A fresh spring salad made with bittercress, pickled ramps bulbs, and feta cheese, waiting to be dressed with Yogurt Bittercress Dressing

Yogurt Bittercress Dressing

Makes about 1 cup

½ cup olive oil
2 Tablespoons lemon juice
1 Tablespoon maple syrup
2 cups washed bittercress greens
1 teaspoon salt
¼ teaspoon ground black pepper
4 field garlic bulbs or 1 clove garlic
½ cup plain yogurt

1. Place all the ingredients in a blender except the yogurt. Blend until smooth.
2. Whisk into the yogurt by hand, otherwise the dressing becomes watery. Drizzle over your favorite salad.

Japanese Knotweed I

Fallopia japonica (*Polygonum cuspidatum*)

Tasting like a cross of a tart fruit and a tangy green vegetable, and looking like bamboo, Japanese knotweed is difficult to classify. As a wild food, it can be delicious with proper preparation in the kitchen.

The fat shoots of Japanese knotweed collected in spring, and the pretty flowers seen in the fall

How to Identify

Japanese knotweed is an herbaceous perennial plant that can grow 4-8 feet tall and in great colonies. The shoots and stalks of knotweed are hollow with swollen nodes or joints that form cross walls between segments. The skin of the stalk toughens with age, and is green mottled with red. The leaves are shaped like a shovel blade; as wide as it is broad, pointed at the tip, and with a flat edge at the base, they can grow to be 4-6 inches long. The leaves emerge from the swollen nodes on the stalk on short stems. The blooms of Japanese knotweed are erect racemes of white or off-white flowers that emerge from the upper leaf axils. They will mature into winged, triangular seeds that may persist through the winter. The stalks will dry up and remain as splintery forests until the following spring, making it easy to recognize where a colony exists and can be visited for foraging in the right season.

Habitat and Range

Japanese knotweed was originally introduced to the United States from Asia as an ornamental plant, but it has spread and become a noxious invasive pest throughout the eastern half of the country, along the west coast up to Alaska, and across several of the Rocky Mountain States. It prefers full sun but will survive in partial shade. Japanese knotweed grows in disturbed soils, along waterways, vacant lots, urban areas, and along roadsides. It spreads through tough underground rhizomes as well as seeds, and collecting some shoots unfortunately will not greatly affect this invasive plant.

When and How to Harvest

The early spring shoots of Japanese knotweed are its only edible parts. Snap off the shoots with your fingers or use a knife to cut shoots that are 8-12 inches tall and whose top leaves are still tightly curled up. As knotweed grows, the skin and stalks become very tough and fibrous, and trying to cook with them will leave you with a dish that seems like it is filled with splinters.

Eating and Preserving

With a similar texture and sour taste as rhubarb, Japanese knotweed is often substituted for rhubarb in dessert recipes like pie. It is best combined with other, sweeter fruit like strawberries to mask some of the green taste from the knotweed. Very young and tender shoots can be peeled and thinly sliced and added raw to grain salads or mixed into recipes for a sour crunch. Chopped and stewed Japanese knotweed shoots can be sweetened and added to muffins or coffee cakes, or hung in a jelly bag to extract a beautiful pink liquid to make an interesting jelly. We have successfully used the traditional Japanese method of salt-preserving young stalks of knotweed to use in later recipes, and they retain their crunch and tartness. Making fruit leather from cooked, sweetened, and pureed knotweed is a good way to use a large amount of the stalks. There is a large amount of resveratrol present in the rhizomes of Japanese knotweed, and commercial supplement makers extract the powerful antioxidant from knotweed as well as grape skins.

Japanese Knotweed Fruit Leather
Makes 2cups puree

4 cups peeled and chopped Japanese knotweed shoots
1 cup water
3 Tablespoons sugar

1. Place the chopped knotweed and water in a large pot and bring the water up to a boil. Reduce to a simmer and stew for 10 minutes, stirring often. The knotweed will change color to light green as it cooks and will start to fall apart.

2. Add the sugar and cook 3 minutes longer. Remove from the heat.

3. Puree the stewed knotweed and allow it to cool. Spread the knotweed puree about 1/8" thick in a dehydrator fruit leather tray or on a silicone baking sheet. Dry at 150° F until the fruit leather changes to a darker green and is dry to the touch, or follow the manufacturer's directions for the dehydrator.

Lamb's Quarters, Goosefoot I, N

Chenopodium album, Chenopodium berlandieri
Lamb's quarters are one of the mildest greens you can add to your diet, foraged for free from the wild or even your own backyard.

A healthy patch of tender lamb's quarters

How to Identify

Lamb's quarters are annual herbaceous plants that can grow up to seven feet tall with branched stalks. The leaves grow alternately on short stems, and are irregularly lobed and approximately diamond shaped, triangular, or shaped similarly to a goose's webbed foot, hence an explanation for one of its many common names. The leaves are often coated with a fine white powder on the underside that is a natural wax the plant produces to protect the leaves from drying out; it can be washed or rubbed off. Lamb's quarters have tiny, green flowers clustered on spikes at the plant's tips that mature to many tiny, black, edible seeds.

Habitat and Range

Two common species of lamb's quarters have different origins, but can hybridize with each other and are equally edible. *Chenopodium album* is originally from Europe, but has become naturalized throughout North America; *Chenopodium berlandieri* is our native lamb's quarters. Both like full to partial sun and disturbed soils, and pop up easily in gardens and at farms, in vacant lots, and roadsides. Lamb's quarters are abundant seed producers and self-seeders, collecting their leaves or seeds will not harm the plant population.

When and How to Harvest

You can gather the tender leaves of lamb's quarters from spring through early fall, snipping them and their short stems from the stem with scissors. Sometimes external environmental factors or the weather will produce slightly purple tinged leaves, which while pretty, we avoid as signs of distress in the plant. To gather the tiny seeds, wait until the seed heads are dry and brown, then crush them between your hands to remove the chaff and expose the dark brown or black seeds. Gently winnow the seeds by blowing away the light chaff, leaving the slightly heavier seeds behind.

Eating and Preserving

The leaves of lamb's quarters are exceptionally mild greens, very similar in flavor to commercially grown baby spinach, and can be used in similar ways. They contain high amounts of fiber, beta-carotene, vitamin C, riboflavin, calcium, zinc, copper, and manganese, along with comparable amounts of oxalic acid as spinach. If you have concerns about oxalic acid consumption because of reduced kidney function, you may want to avoid spinach and lamb's quarters. Use the tender leaves boiled for 2 minutes, steamed, creamed, or sautéed in recipes like omelets, casseroles, pasta dishes, soups, and spanakopita. Lamb's quarters can be collected and lightly boiled or steamed to reduce its volume, then wrung out to remove excess liquid, and frozen in flat-packed plastic bags to use all year long. The seeds can be added to breads for a crunch, or pounded to break open the seed coat and cooked into porridges or ground finely into flour. The whole seeds store well in the freezer. We keep a planter box filled with lamb's quarters near the back steps so we have a constant supply of fresh greens for cooking from spring through autumn. This way it is just steps away from the outdoors to the kitchen to our plates with a wild and nutritious food.

Mallow, Common I ☆

Malva neglecta
Common mallow is a mild tasting plant with several edible parts, and a favorite of kids who like to collect and eat the "cheeses" with their small fingers.

A close-up view of the green seed pod, or "cheese", of common mallow and the scalloped leaves

How to Identify

Common Mallow is a prolific self-seeding herbaceous plant, usually considered an annual, but sometimes persisting through the winter and living as a biennial. The long stems usually lie horizontally along the ground and originate from an off-white tap root. The leaves grow alternately on the main stem on long leaf stems, and are circular to kidney-shaped, 1-2½ inches across, with slightly lobed and toothed edges. The upper and lower surfaces of the leaves and leaf stems are covered with short hairs visible with magnification. The small flowers have five petals and can be white, pinkish, lavender, or striped, and the flowers grow from the leaf axils, often hidden under the leaves. The flowers mature into a schizocarp, which is a fruit that splits up into pieces that hold the seeds, called the "cheese" because it resembles a little wheel of cheese wedges covered in green leaves, which were once the sepals of the flowers.

Habitat and Range

Considered an invasive pest in agricultural fields, common mallow is an invasive weed and can be found throughout most of North America. It grows in lawns, gardens, at roadsides and trail sides, in disturbed areas, and in just about any forgotten area where it can grow in a little dirt. Overcollection is not a concern with this ubiquitous plant.

When and How to Harvest

Mallow leaves can be collected as soon as May and into November before they die back, it is one of the few plants whose greens don't become bitter or tough with age. Just snip the leaf stems off with scissors to collect a large amount of the leaves fairly quickly. The flowers appear in the warmer summer months and can be collected for three months as they don't all open at once. The cheeses are best collected when still bright green and tender, peeling off the leafy green sepals before popping them in your mouth is optional. The roots can be dug in summer and autumn.

Eating and Preserving

The leaves can be eaten raw in salads or added to cooked dishes. Common mallow is related to okra, and exhibits some of the same mucilaginous and thickening properties when cooked. Use the greens in soups, curries, and added to grain salads, they are pleasantly mild. The leaves can also be dried and used in an herbal tisane to relieve coughs. The leaves are rich in vitamins A and C, as well as calcium, magnesium, iron, and selenium. The flowers can be added raw to salads or used as a pretty garnish. The green cheeses are a favorite of kids, and they can pick and eat quite a few of them raw during lazy summer days spent outside. We have read about extracting a mucous-like substance from a root decoction that can be whipped like egg whites, but have yet to try this preparation. The roots can be eaten once boiled, but are rather small.

Milkweed N ☆

Asclepias syriaca

An important food source for Monarch butterflies and foragers alike, milkweed is a wonderful native plant that provides several delicious wild vegetables. Kids can hunt for striped Monarch caterpillars and observe the many other butterflies that are attracted to the flowers, and always enjoy opening the dried seed pods in the autumn to help the fluffy seeds fly away in a breeze.

How to Identify

In the spring, the shoots of milkweed emerge on slender, unbranched stalks that are covered with light fuzz observable under magnification. The leaves grow in opposite pairs, and are 4-9 inches long, oblong ovals with a smooth edge, and are velvety on the undersides. As the season progresses, milkweed will grow 3-6 feet tall and bear several flower umbels from the leaf axils of the top third of the plant. The unopened flower umbels are ball-shaped and look similar to a small

Springtime shoots, summertime flower clusters, and late-summer
green seed pods of milkweed

head of broccoli. The flowers open subsequently, starting with the clusters lower on the stalk, and not all flower clusters will be open at once,
extending the length of time that flowers are available as a food source
for pollinators. The flowers are a mix of pink, white and purple, and
have five petals that bend backwards and lobes that point forward to
make a crown shaped flower, and are fragrant. Not every flower will be
pollinated, but starting in mid-summer through autumn, several from
each cluster will mature into a teardrop-shaped, bumpy seedpod that
will grow to 2-5 inches long and will be filled with flat, teardrop-shaped
seeds that mature to brown and are attached to a silky fluff. All parts of
milkweed exude a white, milky latex when cut. **NOTE**: There are many
varieties and species of cultivated and wild milkweeds, but their edibility is unknown. This entry refers only to common milkweed, *Asclepias
syriaca*. In the spring, milkweed shoots can sometimes be confused
with toxic dogbane, *Apocynum cannabinum*. Milkweed shoots have a
lightly fuzzy stem, while the stem of dogbane is smooth.

Habitat and Range

Common milkweed is native to North America, and can be found in sunny, open areas east of the Rocky Mountains. Milkweed will also grow in fallow fields, along roadsides, in abandoned lots, disturbed areas, and in partial shade. Common milkweed is a perennial plant that spreads by both underground rhizome and through seeds, so established patches will return year after year. Through loss of habitat to development and overuse of pesticides and herbicides, the Monarch population has declined. Collecting small amounts of shoots, unopened flower buds, and seed pods for your personal use will not affect the overall population milkweed, and it has become desirable to plant milkweed in your garden to attract pollinators.

When and How to Harvest

The shoots of common milkweed can be collected from established patches in the spring when they are 6-10 inches tall. Use a knife or scissors to cut them at the bottom of the shoot, but don't collect more than 10%, since you'll want to return and collect parts from the mature plant later in the year. In early summer through mid-summer, the flower clusters can be collected when the flowers are unopened, and the clusters are tight. We don't take more than one cluster from each plant, even though there are many. The opened flowers and unopened flower buds can be collected by snipping them with scissors. The pods start growing in mid-summer and should be collected when they are ½-2 inches long and firm. The immature seeds and fluff inside should be completely white when the pod is opened, otherwise the outer husk will be too tough to eat. Since all parts of milkweed exude the milky latex when cut, we try to shake it off before placing the harvested plant parts in a container, but plan on getting sticky fingers. Also, be on the lookout for Monarch caterpillars hidden in the flower clusters or eggs on the undersides of the leaves. We have accidentally brought home caterpillars and then "fed" our new pets fresh milkweed leaves for a couple weeks or so until the caterpillars grew up, made their chrysalis, and emerged as adult butterflies which we released back into the milk-weed fields. Gillian loves to observe the life cycle of the Monarchs, and has great respect and understanding for their metamorphosis.

One of our Monarch caterpillar friends, eating leaves of common milkweed

Eating and Preserving

The assorted edible parts of milkweed are tender once cooked and have a mild flavor similar to green beans, making them a great addition to many recipes. While many books mistakenly repeat information about boiling milkweed in several changes of water to remove "bitterness", our experiences and reading of newer guide books has shown that common milkweed is never bitter, and does not need multiple boilings in multiple changes of water. It is toxic dogbane that may be confused for milkweed in the shoot stage that is very bitter. If what you have collected as milkweed ever tastes bitter after a quick boiling, it may be a different species of milkweed or dogbane and should not be eaten.

The shoots should be boiled in salted water for 5-10 minutes and can be served plain, with a touch of butter, or covered in a hollandaise sauce. Our favorite parts to eat are the unopened flower buds. They also receive a quick 5-10 minute boil in salted water before incorporating them into quiches, adding them to grain and bean salads, tossing with pastas, baking into casseroles, or pickling them into a caper-like condiment. The flowers can have their fragrance and nectar infused into liquors or deep-fried into fritters, and will also lightly color and flavor a sun tea. The pods are another great vegetable, with a built-in place to stuff with all kinds of fillings and bake. Give the larger 2 inch pods a quick boil and then open them along the natural split that runs the length of the pod on one side. Scoop out the immature white seeds and fluff (but don't discard it, since it is another edible part!) and stuff with cream cheese and jalapenos, cooked rice and vegetables, seasoned breadcrumbs and sautéed mushrooms, or any other yummy filling, and bake the stuffed pods for tasty wild appetizers. Use the immature seeds and fluff in casseroles and rice dishes; it adds a nice sweetness and texture. The shoots, unopened flower buds, and tender milkweed pods can be blanched and frozen to use later, and the larger opened flower buds or very small seedpods can be pickled or lacto-fermented and kept in the refrigerator as a condiment.

Milkweed Pods and Chickpea Salad
Makes about 3 cups

2 cups small milkweed pods, about 1-1½" long
1–16 oz. can chickpeas, drained
¼ red onion, sliced thinly
¼ cup crumbled feta cheese

Dressing:

3 Tablespoons red wine vinegar
1 Tablespoon fresh basil, chopped
¼ teaspoon salt

¼ teaspoon pepper
½ teaspoon sugar
1 clove garlic, minced
2 Tablespoons olive oil

1. Scrub the milkweed pods, and boil them for 5 minutes. Shock them in ice water. Slice the stem ends off the pods and slice them in half, removing the seeds and silk.
2. Toss the milkweed pods with the chickpeas, onions, and feta cheese.
3. To make the dressing, whisk the vinegar, chopped basil, salt, pepper, sugar and garlic together in a bowl. While whisking, drizzle in the olive oil slowly, making an emulsion. Toss the salad with the dressing, and refrigerate for at least an hour before serving.

Nettles N, I

Urtica dioica, Urtica gracilis
If you can avoid the sting from stinging nettles, you'll be awarded with a nutrient dense, free green that tastes deeply earthy, green, and

delicious. Watch the kids around the nettles; while the sting is temporary, it hurts!

A field of nettles, and a close-up showing the toothed leaves and stinging hairs

How to Identify

Nettles are an herbaceous perennial that grow from 3-7 feet tall, dying back in the winter. The leaves grow oppositely in pairs, have a strongly toothed edge and papery texture, and taper to a long point with a heart-shaped base. The stem is tough and stringy, indicating one of its traditional uses for making cording and textiles. The stems, leaf stems, and leaves of nettles are covered with stinging hairs that produce a burning itch if rubbed against, although the North American nettle has less of the stinging hairs. Small green flowers hang from the leaf axils of female plants, while male flowers are diagonally erect at the tops of male plants.

Habitat and Range

The native North American nettle (*Urtica gracilis*) and the naturalized European nettle (*Urtica dioica*) both grow in rich soil, disturbed areas, moist woodlands, along rivers, and in old fields throughout North America with the exception of Nevada. Nettles will tolerate some shade and prefer full sun. Collecting the new growth of leaves from the tops of nettle plants will not affect a population as nettles spread in colonies through underground rhizomes and by prolific seeding.

When and How to Harvest

Nettles are best harvested when their tops are still tender and growing in the spring. Once they start flowering in the summer, they become too stringy and produce compounds called cystoliths that can irritate your urinary tract if eaten. We harvest nettles from a large field with gardening gloves and scissors into large buckets, although Robert can use his ungloved fingers to pinch them off after practicing a method where he quickly picks with an upward motion that prevents the hairs from stinging. We are only taking the top 3-5 inches of the stems and leaves in the spring, although sometimes in the fall a second flush of nettles will regrow and we can gather more then.

Eating and Preserving

There have been many times we have painfully stumbled into a nettle patch by accident, and the threat of a burning sting may have you wondering why I would recommend searching for nettles as a wild food. *Cooking or dehydrating stinging nettles neutralizes the sting making nettles safe for consumption.* Nettles are high in iron, calcium, protein, and vitamins C and A, and make an excellent cooked green. We add them fresh to soups and add lightly cooked nettles to quiche, risottos, and Indian dishes like *saag* in place of spinach. We also dry a lot of the leaves to use for steeped hot tisanes in winter, and powdered as a seasoning by adding the green powder to breads and pasta doughs. For their nutrition and their great taste, we recommend nettles as a free superfood to any foraging family.

Nettle Soup with Lentils

Makes about 6 servings

2 Tablespoons olive oil
1 large onion, diced

⅓ cup dry lentils
2 teaspoons turmeric
3 cups vegetable broth
3 cups water
10 oz. fresh nettle leaves, cleaned
About 20 ramps leaves and stems, chopped, or use ½ cup chopped scallions
½ cup dry linguine, broken into pieces
1 cup plain yogurt

1. Heat the oil and sauté the onions over medium heat until browned.
2. Add lentils and turmeric and sauté 1 minute. Pour in vegetable broth and water and bring to a boil, reduce to medium and cook 10 minutes.
3. Add nettles and ramps or scallions, simmer 20 minutes longer.
4. Stir in pasta pieces, and cook 10 minutes longer, until the pasta is al dente. The broth should be a deep, greenish-yellow.
5. Ladle soup into bowls and serve with a dollop of yogurt.

Purslane I

Portulaca oleracea

Kids can easily identify this mildly sour, crunchy green that you likely have growing in the garden. Trendy restaurants will serve purslane, and farmer's markets will try to sell it to you, but you can collect your own gourmet wild edible right outside the back door.

Reddish stemmed purslane creeps along the ground with
its succulent green leaves

How to Identify

Purslane is an annual succulent plant that spreads horizontally with branching clusters of paddle-shaped, fleshy leaves. The thick stems are tinged red and can grow 4-10 inches long. Purslane's small yellow flowers have five petals and are hidden between the branched stems, only opening for a brief period in the morning. The flowers mature into fruit capsules whose tops will fall off in late summer to reveal numerous, tiny black seeds.

Habitat and Range

Purslane is considered an invasive weed in some areas; it has been naturalized throughout North America, originally from North Africa and the Middle East, and grown as a common garden vegetable in Europe. It grows in sunny, sandy soils in cultivated fields of farms, in disturbed soils, between flagstones in paths, and likely in your own garden or flower pots outside. Instead of pulling all of the purslane as a weed, let it mature enough to drop its seeds and continually produce a small patch within your reach.

When and How to Harvest

Purslane appears in late spring and dies back in the fall. It is surprisingly drought resistant and can handle the heat of summer. Just break off a few stems and give them a quick wash before using purslane as a succulent vegetable.

Eating and Preserving

Purslane leaves make beautiful edible garnishes, and I often add a few young tops to Gillian's school lunches. Since they are available most of the year, we just use purslane fresh, although we have made quick refrigerator pickles with some of the larger stems and leaves. Add them to green salads or mixed grain salads raw, or lightly cook them in soups. Purslane provides iron, beta-carotene, and some omega-3 fatty acids in a tasty, free green vegetable.

Ramps, Wild Leeks N ☆

Allium tricoccum, Allium burdickii
A culinary darling, ramps are a highly sought-after wild edible. They are a traditional spring food of the Appalachian region and are celebrated each year with festivals. We love to utilize their greens, which have the same funky/pungent/garlicky flavor of the bulbs and are quite easy to collect.

How to Identify

Ramps have broad, smooth edged, waxy green leaves that are 4-12 inches long and have parallel veins that run the length of the leaves. Two or three leaves will grow from the bulb on stalks that are tinged

The forest floor carpeted with edible and delicious ramps greens

Young ramps bulbs and the flower umbel

with red or purple in common ramps (*Allium tricoccum*) or are all white in narrow-leaved ramps (*Allium burdickii*). They often grow in tight clumps of plants that may benefit from some selective thinning. The bulb is white, oblong, and perennial, with stringy white roots attached to the bottom. White, six petaled flowers are arranged in an umbrella-like cluster at the top of an unbranched, smooth stalk that emerges from the center of the bulb. The flowers produce round, hard, black seeds in clumps of three that may persist through the winter. All parts of the fresh plant will produce an oniony-garlicky smell when crushed, an important identifying factor.

Habitat and Range

Ramps prefer moist, partially shaded, rich woodlands and will some-times appear to carpet the forest floor in green leaves. They range from eastern Canada through the Great Lakes region, south to the higher elevations of Georgia, and all along the east coast. Ramps may sometimes appear locally abundant, but in a few states they are listed as commercially exploited and their status is of special concern; check the status of ramps for your area. Careful and selective collecting of ramps is highly suggested—only collect from lush patches, don't collect more than 10 percent of a patch, and collect only what you will use, keeping in mind that taking the bulb kills the entire plant.

When and How to Harvest

Fancy restaurants want the young flush of green leaves and the attached bulb to showcase in recipes in spring. Sometimes they even remove and throw away the greens, which we think is shameful. Taking the entire plant is a lethal collection for the plant. Ramps are very slow reproducers, mostly spreading through perennial bulb division and less often through self-seeding. The leaves are in good shape for about six weeks in April and May, and then they will start to yellow and die back when the flower stalk appears. We collect and use the leaves of ramps, only cutting one of the leaves from each plant and leaving the other leaves and bulb alone. In large patches, a bag of aromatic leaves can easily be collected with scissors or by grasping and pulling a single leaf in a short amount of time, leaving all the bulbs intact. We only dig the bulbs in the fall with a small garden shovel if we have a very specific recipe or use for them in mind, after the greens and flowers have died back and all of the plant's energy has gone back into the bulb to survive the winter. The bulbs of the spring ramps, often with the leaves still attached, are small and slender, while the bulbs dug in the fall are large and plump.

Eating and Preserving

The wonderful flavor of the bulb is present in the leaves, along with some nutritious vitamin A, vitamin C, and selenium. In the spring, we cook just about everything with some chopped ramps greens tossed in for ramp-y flavor—soups, grains, casseroles, pizza, eggs, and everything else. The greens can be dehydrated and powdered to add to breads and pasta dough, or the raw greens can be chopped and frozen, tightly packed in containers to use all year in cooked dishes. We love to make a pesto from the raw greens of ramps; it also freezes well in small containers and can be used all year to make breadstick twists for wild foods potluck, or added to pizzas and pasta for dinner. Two recipes for which we are willing to dig some of the bulbs are pickled ramps and a savory ramps jam, both excellent accompaniments to sandwiches.

Ramps Pesto and Breadstick Twists
Makes about 24 twists

For the pesto:

   2 cups washed and coarsely chopped ramps greens
   ½ teaspoon salt
   2 Tablespoons pine nuts

¼ cup grated hard cheese, like Parmesan
2 Tablespoons olive oil

1. Place all the ingredients except the olive oil into a food processor and pulse until finely chopped. Slowly drizzle in the olive oil until a thick paste forms. You will have about a half cup of pesto.

For the dough:

7 oz. warm water
1 teaspoon sugar
1½ teaspoons instant dried yeast
3 cups flour
2 tablespoons olive oil
1 teaspoon salt
1 cup shredded mozzarella cheese
1 egg, beaten with 1 Tablespoon water for egg wash
Sesame seeds (optional)

1. Pour the warm water into a large mixing bowl and dissolve the sugar and yeast in it. Allow the yeast to start foaming, about 8 minutes.
2. With a wooden spoon, mix in the first cup of flour, and then add the oil and salt. Add another 1½ cups of flour, mixing vigorously with the spoon, or use the dough hook attachment of a stand mixer.
3. Sprinkle the remaining ½ cup of flour on a surface and knead the dough for a few minutes, until it becomes smooth. Add enough flour to your surface and hands to keep the dough from sticking to you. When the dough is smooth and springy, place it into a greased bowl, cover it with a damp towel or plastic wrap, and let it rise in a warm place for 1 hour. It will double in volume.
4. Heat your oven to 400° F.
5. Punch down the dough to deflate it. Roll the dough on a floured surface into a 12 inch by 12 inches square. Spread the pesto on the

lower half of the square, and then evenly sprinkle the shredded mozzarella cheese over the pesto. Fold the empty top half of the dough square over the cheese and pesto, pressing it together, with the pesto and cheese inside the dough "envelope". The melting cheese will act like a glue to keep the halves together.

6. Using a pizza cutter, cut strips about ½ inch wide through both layers of dough, with the pesto sandwiched in the middle. Give them a quick twist before placing them on a parchment covered sheet pan. Brush with the egg wash, sprinkle with sesame seeds if you are using them, and allow the twists to rest for 20 minutes. Bake for 18-22 minutes, until browned.

Sheep Sorrel I

Rumex acetosella
With that tart and sour flavor that kids seem to love, sheep sorrel is a natural addition to their trailside nibbling and your dinner salads.

A lush patch and some perfect specimens of sheep sorrel

How to Identify

Sheep sorrel is a perennial herb with arrow-shaped leaves whose lower lobes are elongated and pulled outwards; if you hold a leaf upside-down, you can see the sheep's head shape with the bulbous face and lobes as the sheep's ears. The leaves can grow 1-3 inches long on slightly grooved stems growing from a basal rosette. Sheep sorrel produces flower stalks up to 14 inches in length bearing loosely branched spikes of red and green flowers in early summer.

Habitat and Range

Sheep sorrel grows in disturbed soil, in garden beds, in lawns, and in sandy, acidic soils. It prefers full sun, but will survive in partial shade. Originally from Europe and Asia, it is now considered naturalized throughout North America, although many commercial farmers still consider it a noxious pest. Sheep sorrel readily spreads through underground roots and seeds, so overharvest is not a problem.

When and How to Harvest

Sheep sorrel is in season from spring until fall. Use scissors to cut off clumps of green leaves from the basal rosette before the plants flower, and avoid any red-tinged leaves as they will be slightly bitter. The stems can be a bit stringy, so you'll want to remove them before eating the leaves raw or cooking them. Fresh sheep sorrel can be stored in a plastic bag in the refrigerator for a few days.

Eating and Preserving

The leaves of sheep sorrel are quite tender and make nice, tart additions to salads or salad dressings due to the oxalic acid present. We also add the leaves to sandwiches and grain salads. Sheep sorrel can be cooked in soups or made into acidic sauces, but will lose its fresh green color and turn more of a drab olive green. Keep in mind that the leaves will lose a great deal of volume once de-stemmed and cooked. While out camping one spring, friends caught some lovely brook trout and we cooked them in foil over the campfire, stuffed with sheep sorrel found next to the tents, lending their lemony flavor to the yummy fish. We mostly snack on fresh sheep sorrel as a nibble while out hiking; it is an easy green for kids to identify on their own, and they happily refer to it as "sour grass".

Spicebush N

Lindera benzoin
Another of the aromatic scratch-and-sniff wild edibles we gather, spicebush twigs and leaves can be collected along with their ripe berries to add an unexpected, exotic zing to recipes.

Spicebush leaves, twigs, and ripe berries

How to Identify

Spicebush is a medium sized deciduous shrub growing from 3-15 feet tall in rich woodlands. Its leaves are alternate, simple, oval-shaped with pointed tips, smooth edges, and grow 2-6 inches long. The twigs and bark are greyish-brown and speckled with lenticels. Before the leaves appear in the spring, spicebushes produce their dense clusters of tiny, yellow flowers at the leaf axils. The flowers of the female bushes, once cross pollinated by the flowers of the male bushes, develop into oval-shaped berries, about ¼- ½ inch long, bright green ripening to red in autumn, with one edible, oval, black seed inside. The twigs, leaves, and berries all have a spicy-citrus flavor when crushed or scratched.

Habitat and Range

Spicebush shrubs often grow in colonies in the understory of established, partially shaded, moist forests, and along stream banks and the lower slopes of mountains. They are native to North America and range from New York and Ontario south to Texas and Florida, and all along the east coast. Spicebush shrubs are an important food source for the Spicebush Swallowtail butterfly, and many birds eat and spread the ripe seeds of spicebushes. In its range, collection of spicebush is a special concern only in Maine, otherwise feel free to collect a small amount of leaves, twigs, or berries from a large colony of spicebushes.

When and How to Harvest

The twigs of spicebush can be harvested at any time of the year, including the winter, by cutting or breaking them off. Leaves are best collected while they are bright green. The berries will ripen to red in autumn and disappear quickly, so grab some when you see them by picking them into hard containers.

Spicebush ice cream

Eating and Preserving

The different parts of spicebush have slightly different flavors and uses. The leaves have a very citrusy flavor, and make a refreshing cold-steeped drink; the leaves are best used freshly picked, as they don't dry well. The twigs have more of an allspice/citrus flavor, and can be used all year to make a hot, brewed drink for cold winter days, or as flavored skewers for grilled meats. I like to nibble on a peeled twig while we walk in the woods. The berries have the strongest flavor of the whole bush, almost too intense to eat alone, spicy and peppery, with a slight citrus edge. We crush and add them to cooked applesauce and home-canned fruits like apples and pears, flavor sugar for baking, and infuse them in cream for custards and ice cream. For the adults, we infuse liquors with the twigs and berries for flavored spirits. Keep a jar of whole, ripe spicebush berries in the freezer; because of their high oil content they don't dry well and will go rancid at room temperature. The berries will darken once frozen, but retain their flavor and aroma for recipes.

Wood Sorrel N

Oxalis stricta, Oxalis species
Pretty and sour, and another favorite yard nibble for the kids, wood sorrel is easy to identify. Consider keeping this weed in your yard or garden for a quick addition to home-cooked meals as an acidic component or just a pretty garnish.

Wood sorrel grows conveniently next to the house, with its heart-shaped leaves and pretty yellow flowers

How to Identify

Wood sorrel is an herbaceous annual plant often considered a weed. Each alternate leaf is composed of three delicate, heart-shaped leaflets on a long, slender stem that curl up at night and reopen during the day. The small five petaled flowers of common wood sorrel (*Oxalis stricta*) are yellow, and other species of wood sorrels have different colored flowers from violet (*Oxalis violacea*) to a white and pink striped mountain sorrel (*Oxalis montana*). Wood sorrel's seedpods are slightly hairy, elongated, and ridged, standing erect on the flower stems, and explosively disperse the seeds when touched.

Habitat and Range

Wood sorrel prefers partial sunlight, but will grow in full sun, with the leaflets seemingly wilting during the hottest part of the day. It grows in disturbed soil, in gardens, in lawns, and alkaline soils. Wood sorrel is native to most of North America, and grows just about everywhere except Hawaii, Alaska, California, Oregon, Nevada and Utah. Wood sorrel spreads prolifically through seeds, so collecting this common little weed won't hurt the population.

When and How to Harvest

Wood sorrel leaflets are ready to harvest at any time from mid-spring to early fall, and are easily pulled off their long, stringy stems with your hands. The flowers and the immature seedpods are edible as well.

Eating and Preserving

Oxalic acid is what gives wood sorrel its sour zing, and Gillian re-named it "Lemony" while gathering and eating it. Add raw leaves, flowers, and immature seedpods to green salads and mixed grain salads. I garnish rice with the heart-shaped leaves, removing them from their long stems, washing and patting them dry before sprinkling them around. Wood sorrel is one of the easiest and most satisfying wild foods to show to new learners because the taste of lemons is just so unexpected, and its shape is very distinct. Wood sorrel can also be added to soups and lightly cooked into sauces, but it will lose its bright green color and turn a drab green. The oxalic acid is only a limiting factor for people with compromised kidney functions; wood sorrel has less oxalic acid than commercially grown spinach. As with all new or wild foods, eat just a small amount at a time.

CHAPTER 9:

Foraging and Digging Roots

OK folks, it's time to let the kids get dirty. We're going to get out the shovel and gloves, and search for the roots, tubers, rhizomes, and bulbs of wild plants that are edible. Are you concerned about eating something dug from the ground? If you eat carrots, potatoes, turnips, radishes, onions, beets, or ginger, you are already using the edible underground parts of plants. True roots and similar underground elements are storage organs of plants; enlarged to store energy for the plant in the form of carbohydrates, starches, and sugars during cooler months when the rest of the plant is dormant.

When environmental conditions are favorable, the plant utilizes the energy stored in the root to put out greens and flowers, so the energy in the roots is depleted. Digging for many roots should be done when the plant is dormant; either in the fall right before cold weather or in early spring before the plant starts actively growing again. Some roots, like those of sassafras, can be pulled up at any time, while roots of biennials should be dug in the plant's first year before it becomes too woody and tough. If you want to dig the roots while the above ground parts of a plant are dormant, you will have to already know where a population of plants is growing, which is why it is important to recognize plants during several seasons. Keep in mind that digging and collecting the roots of plants is often a lethal collection killing the entire plant, and should be used only on healthy and abundant plant colonies. A few plants will benefit from a selective thinning of dense populations, and some plants can regrow from broken off bits of the roots left in the ground.

There are several names for the different underground organs of plants, but they perform many of the same functions as true roots: anchoring the plant in the soil, absorbing water and minerals from the soil, and storing energy for the plant. *Tap roots* are thickened, fleshy roots that usually grow straight down into the ground, sometimes branching and covered with smaller, fibrous roots that help with water and mineral absorption. Primary roots that branch out into many smaller roots that are swollen are called *tubers*, like the potato. Other underground organs are rootstocks, which are actually underground stems that produce leaves and function the same ways as true roots. A *rhizome* is an underground, horizontal stem that produces fine roots from swollen nodes. A *corm* is the enlarged base of the plant's stem, while a *bulb* is a storage organ made up of thickened scales growing in layers, like an onion. Some roots of plants or trees can form symbiotic relationships with bacteria that allow the plant to fix nitrogen in poor soils, and other roots form mycorrhizal relationships with fungi that benefit both the plant and the fungi.

We collect the roots of plants to benefit from the stored starches and carbohydrates of the plant. Most of the roots we dig are used like our common root vegetables; in stews and soups, pureed, mashed, or as a flavoring agent.

The roots of these other plants are edible, but discussed and identified in more detail in other sections of this book because of their additional, more useful parts:

- Cattail
- Daylily
- Dandelion
- Garlic Mustard
- Mallow
- Ramps

Burdock I ☆

Arctium lappa, Arctium minus
You might first notice burdock by its burrs that get stuck to your socks or dog's fur while out hiking, but soon come to see it as a valuable food source for its roots and edible flower stalks.

How to Identify

Burdock is a biennial herbaceous plant that grows in a basal rosette from a large creamy white taproot with brown, bark-like skin. The

Taproots of first year burdock, and those hooked burrs that stick to your socks

leaves of the first year burdock grow directly from the taproot on long stems, are slightly wooly on their undersides, shaped like elongated hearts up to 28 inches long, with a ruffled edge, and are rather rough and coarse. The leaf stems of great burdock (*Arctium lappa*) are solid, while leaf stems of common burdock (*Arctium minus*) are hollow. In burdock's second year, it produces the flower stalk from the center of the basal rosette, and the flower stalk can grow from 2-9 feet tall, with alternating, smaller leaves, stringy skin, and long flower stems branching from the stalk. The flowers are dark pink to purple, made up of many small florets and hooked bracts, which dry into the globular burr that gets caught on your clothes.

Habitat and Range

Burdocks are originally from Europe, and have become naturalized throughout most of North America. They like partially sunny to sunny spots in nitrogen-rich soil. Burdock grows in disturbed soil, in backyards, empty lots, in the compost pile, at farms, and in gardens. Harvesting the roots of first year burdock or the flower stalks of the second year plants will not affect the overall populations of burdock because of the large amount of seeds it produces, but consider letting some first year plants mature to grow their flower stalk the following year.

Second year burdock and first year burdock growing together

When and How to Harvest

The root of burdock should be collected in its first year of growth before it sends up the flower stalk, best dug in the fall or very early spring; the second year roots will be stringy and tough. Burdock root may require quite a bit of digging with something larger than a garden trowel, as the root can grow up to 4 feet long. Clean the dirt from the roots with a stiff brush, or peel it with a potato peeler. We collect the fattest flower stalks from burdock before the flowers appear, in early to mid-spring, by cutting the 2-9 foot tall flower stalk at the base and cutting the leaves off and discarding them. The thicker the flower stalk, the more edible vegetable you will have once it is peeled.

Eating and Preserving

The Japanese adore burdock root, and cultivate it as a vegetable called *gobo*. Sometimes we can even find burdock root in the local Asian markets, long, thin, and unbranched. Wild burdock has a slightly stronger flavor than the cultivated vegetable, tasting a bit sweet and nutty. Add sliced burdock root to soups and stews, thinly sliced to vegetable stir-fries, or boiled and mashed like potatoes. We make refrigerator pickles from the lightly boiled roots, and have pureed the cooked roots into a paste to dehydrate into gluten-free chips. The flower stalks are a more tender vegetable part of the burdock plant. You'll have to peel the flower stalk, but the peel comes off in relatively large, stringy pieces, leaving the tender, light green core behind. Lightly steamed or boiled for 5 minutes, it tastes like artichokes. We eat them plain with a bit of butter and salt, rolled into vegetarian sushi, or add the chopped flower stalks to rice pilaf or baked into casseroles. Burdock root contains high amounts of carbohydrates, vitamins B, C, and E, potassium, and manganese.

Chicory, Blue Sailors I

Cichorium intybus

This common roadside weed grows from a taproot that can be made into a caffeine-free coffee substitute; a favorite New Orleans-style brew contains roasted chicory blended with coffee for a darker, sweet and spicy flavor.

Blue flowers and thick roots of chicory

How to Identify

Chicory is a perennial plant that grows from a basal rosette in early spring directly from the taproot. Its basal leaves are deeply toothed, about 3-6 inches long, have a reddish midrib, and irregular hairs. From late spring through early fall, a branched, tough, and hairy flower stalk grows up to 4 feet tall, bearing 15-20 flower heads. The leaves along the flower stalk clasp the stalk, and get progressively smaller the higher up the flower stalk they grow. The flower is a pretty blue, sometimes white or pinkish in color, with two rows of fringed ray flowers that look like petals. Not all of the flowers open at once, and they wither after opening for one day. The overall appearance of chicory is of a scraggly weed. The taproot is stiff and sometimes branched, beige on the outside and white on the inside.

Habitat and Range

Chicory is originally from Europe, but has naturalized throughout the lower 48 states of North America; it is sometimes considered an invasive pest. It grows in disturbed areas, along highway medians and roadsides, in fallow fields, and prefers full sun. Collecting the roots of chicory will not impact the often large colonies of this overlooked weed.

When and How to Harvest

The leaves of chicory can be collected in early spring and eaten as greens. The opened flowers should be picked in the mornings or early afternoon before they wilt. The taproot can be dug all year with a small shovel or garden trowel.

Eating and Preserving

Chicory greens are cultivated and eaten by the Italians, Spanish, Greeks, and French in traditional meals, cooking the greens and combining them with pastas or garlic and fava beans. Wild chicory leaves can be used in similar ways if they are gathered in spring before they become too bitter; some of the bitterness can be reduced by boiling the greens and discarding the cooking water before adding them to recipes. The flowers make nice edible garnishes or additions to salads when pulled apart, but they will also impart some bitter flavors. The taproot of chicory is its most flavorful part, roasted and ground into a coffee substitute or coffee extender. Scrub the roots with a brush to remove the dirt, chop the roots into chunks, and roast it slowly in a 300 degree oven for 2-4 hours until they are dark and dry. Then grind up the roasted root in a coffee grinder, and brew up a rich, dark brew with a bit of sweetener and steamed milk.

Field Garlic I ☆

Allium vineale
Wild garlic that grows freely in your yard, field garlic makes a fantastic and free addition to many meals. Kids will cheerfully nibble on this "onion grass", which they can easily identify by its characteristic smell.

Sometimes the only green thing in a brown lawn, field garlic
can be easily pulled up to use like chives

How to Identify

The leaves of perennial field garlic can grow up to 3 feet tall from the bulb, and are tender, hollow tubes when young, becoming slightly ridged and tougher with age. Field garlic often grows in large clumps of many bulbs and leaves. The flower stalk is tall, stiff, and slender, with a single globular, umbrella-shaped flower head of many light purple, 6 petaled flowers. Sometimes instead of producing flowers, the stalk will produce a globular cluster of small, greenish-white bulblets that will fall to the ground to produce more plants in the fall. The underground bulb looks like really small cultivated garlic bulbs, divided into several cloves that are covered with a papery outer skin. *Note*: All parts of field garlic must have the oniony-garlicky smell for proper identification, and all parts are edible.

Habitat and Range

Field garlic is native to Europe and is considered an invasive plant in North America, ranging along the eastern half of the United States and Canada, and from Alaska along the west coast into California. It prefers full sun and will grow in lawns, backyards, disturbed soil, open fields, and sometimes in clumps in open woods. Digging the bulbs for consumption will not affect the overall population of this invasive pest.

When and How to Harvest

Field garlic can be found between the fall and spring months, often persisting all winter, even when there is a bit of snow on the ground; during the warm summer months, the leaves of field garlic die back. It looks like a cluster of tall, bright green grass against the brown and dead grass of lawns, the reason some people name them "yard onions". To use the hollow leaves, cut the thinnest and most tender leaves in bundles with scissors and give them a rinse. To collect the largest underground bulbs, you'll want to find the thickest and largest leaves in a cluster, and gently loosen the dirt around the bulbs and pull them up whole. Overall, the bulbs don't get very large, and we sometimes collect the smaller bulbs to use more like scallions. The flowers and tiny bulblets on the top of the flower stalk are easily picked by cutting or snapping the whole flower stalk off.

Eating and Preserving

The tender and young new growth of leaves can be finely chopped and used in many similar ways like chives in recipes. We chop and dehydrate some of the leaves to use in recipes all year, and sometimes powder the dried leaves to flavor pasta dough, vegetable broth, and breads. The small cloves of the bulbs can difficult to peel, but small fingers of children will make quick work of it; you can also use a garlic press to squeeze the flesh from the peels. We pull up some of the smaller bulbs, and Gillian loves to eat them grilled whole with a bit of olive oil and salt. They make tasty additions to sandwiches and grains, becoming sweeter as they caramelize. The pretty purple flowers are edible, and can be added to salads for a mild, oniony kick. We make flavored oils or vinegar by infusing them with the small bulblets, lightly crushed, in glass jars. While some people will consider field garlic a weed and apply chemicals to their lawns to try to kill it, a smart foraging family will embrace its existence as food!

Cottage Cheese and Field Garlic Bread
Makes one 8" x 4" loaf

½ cup warm water
1 teaspoon sugar
1½ teaspoons active dry yeast (about half an envelope)
1 cup small curd cottage cheese

½ cup chopped field garlic
1 egg
1 teaspoon salt
¼ teaspoon baking soda
1 cup whole wheat flour
1 cup all-purpose flour

1. In a large bowl, mix together the warm water, sugar, and yeast. Let it sit for 15 minutes until the yeast is foamy and active.

2. In a small saucepan, warm the cottage cheese up to room temperature. Add the chopped field garlic, and add to the yeast mixture in the large bowl.

3. With a large spoon, mix in the egg, salt, baking soda, and flours into the yeas and cottage cheese mixture. Mix until there is no more dry flour visible. The batter will be thick, but too wet to knead.

4. Cover the bowl and let it sit in a warm place for 1½ hours to proof.

5. Heat the oven to 350° F. Grease an 8" x 4" loaf pan, and pour the bread batter into the pan, spreading it evenly.

6. Let the loaf rise for about an hour, or until the loaf has doubled in size. Bake for 30-40 minutes, until the loaf is browned. Cool for 20 minutes and remove the loaf from the pan. Serve the bread sliced, toasted, and smeared with cream cheese.

Indian Cucumber N

Medeola virginiana

Even though they look like fat grubs, the rhizomes of Indian cucumber are sweet and crunchy treats for kids. Collected conscientiously, they can be a novel addition to a young wild food forager's knowledge.

How to Identify

Indian cucumbers are perennial plants that grow from their underground rhizome on a single stalk that is covered with a cottony fiber

Indian cucumber stalk with the second tier of leaves and
flower, and the sweet rhizome

along its base. It can grow either a single or double tier of whorled
leaves, based upon the age of the plant. The lower tier of leaves are
lance-shaped, waxy, smooth edged, 3-4 inches long, and growing in a
whorl of 5-9 leaves, while the upper tier of leaves are shorter and only
produce 3-5 leaves. From the upper tier of leaves, a cluster of light yellow, downward growing flowers blooms in the spring, maturing into
bluish-black, 6 seeded berries in autumn. The underground rhizome
grows horizontally, thickest near the base of the stem and tapering to

a point at the end, with many thin, hairy roots attached to its length. The rhizome is waxy, white, and crunchy, and will snap cleanly into smaller pieces.

Habitat and Range

Indian cucumber is native to North America and occurs in rich, slightly acidic, mixed forests from Minnesota south to Louisiana, and all along the eastern side of the continent. Indian cucumber is considered endangered in Florida and Illinois, so should not be collected in those states. While local populations may seem abundant, it is best to collect Indian cucumber in very small quantities, as digging the rhizome is a lethal collection and will kill an individual plant.

When and How to Harvest

The only edible part of the Indian cucumber is its underground rhizome. It can be collected any time during the spring, summer, or fall when you encounter a robust population of Indian cucumber plants, remembering to harvest no more than 10 percent of the rhizomes. The rhizome must be dug up; the stem pops off very easily if pulled, and remember that it grows horizontally and not straight downwards. We carry some water with us, and just rinse the rhizome off before eating it on the spot. The plants with the double tier of leaves tend to yield larger rhizomes.

Eating and Preserving

Because of their slow growth and sometimes sparse populations, we don't dig enough Indian cucumber to use in recipes, but dig a few while out hiking as a refreshing treat. The rhizome is very crisp and sweet, with a resemblance to cucumbers and their cool, firm texture and taste. The plant's appearance is distinct enough that kids can easily recognize them, and will be rewarded for their sharp observation skills with the sweet crunch of a tasty wild food.

Sassafras N

Sassafras albidum

One of the scratch-and-sniff wild plants, sassafras is a traditional source of root beer, a flavored hot tea, and culinary filé powder for Cajun and Creole cooking. Kids will like to find all the differently shaped leaves of a sassafras tree, especially the one shaped like a dinosaur's foot!

Notice the three distinct shapes of the leaves of sassafras, and you can easily pull up their fragrant roots

How to Identify

Sassafras is a deciduous tree growing up to eighty feet tall under the right conditions, but is often smaller and spindly. The bark of mature tree trunks is deeply furrowed and dark reddish-brown, while the bark of the young saplings and twigs is green. Sassafras trees have three, smooth edged, differently shaped leaves present on the tree: a simple oval leaf, a bi-lobed leaf that looks like a mitten, and a tri-lobed leaf. Small, yellowish-green flowers bloom in early spring before the leaves appear, which mature into small, non-edible black fruits held by a cup-shaped stem in late summer. The roots of sassafras grow horizontally and sometimes shallowly, producing root sprouts which develop into many saplings and new trees in abundance from one large, mother tree. All parts of the sassafras tree will have a pleasant, spicy aroma if scratched or crushed.

Habitat and Range

Sassafras is a tree native to eastern North America, growing east from Iowa and south to Texas. It grows in partially shaded deciduous hardwood forests in rich, well-drained soil. A colony of clones can be produced through underground root sprouts from one large tree, many of which will not survive under the leaf canopy. Collecting some leaves and pulling up the saplings will not negatively affect the overall population of sassafras.

When and How to Harvest

The leaves of sassafras can be collected any time while they are still green. The aromatic roots and inner bark can be collected any time the ground is not frozen. We easily spot the saplings that grow in large groups by noticing their green bark and upturned branches even in spring before they have leafed out, and can slowly pull up any sapling about 2 feet tall or smaller. The most aromatic part is the inner bark of the root, which we shave off using a knife once the root has been scrubbed clean.

Eating and Preserving

To use the leaves as filé seasoning, dry them and grind them in a coffee grinder into a fine powder. Filé powder is used as a thickener for sauces and stews like gumbo. To make the traditional orange-colored sassafras "tea", we make a decoction of chopped fresh or dried roots, simmered in water for about 20 minutes and lightly sweetened with honey. We keep some chopped and dehydrated sassafras roots in the house to make this warm beverage all winter long, since both Robert and Gillian enjoy it so much. A traditional root beer can be made from sassafras root, only mildly alcoholic using beer yeast to create the carbonation. A non-alcoholic carbonated beverage can be made by adding seltzer water to a stronger decoction of the roots. *Note*: While the FDA has banned the use of safrol oil, which is extracted from sassafras, as a dangerous carcinogenic compound, we feel that the consumption of reasonable amounts of sassafras tea is safe.

Sassafras Root Beer

Makes about 4, 1 quart bottles

¼ lb. fresh sassafras root
1 gallon water
22 oz. granulated sugar
½ oz. fresh or frozen spicebush berries (optional)
2 Tablespoons lemon or lime juice
1¼ teaspoons beer yeast

For the bottling:

4 teaspoons raw turbinado sugar

1. Boil the fresh sassafras roots with the water for 20 minutes. Remove from heat and add the sugar, spicebush berries, and lime juice. Allow the mixture to cool to 90°F.

2. Remove a cup of the lukewarm water and sprinkle the yeast over the top, allowing it to dissolve and become a bit foamy. Pour the yeast mixture and the remaining decoction into a 1 gallon glass jar fitted with an airlock. Ferment for 3 days.

3. Strain the roots and berries from the beer. To the bottom of each sanitized lock-top bottle, add one teaspoon of raw turbinado sugar. Pour in 4 cups of the beer, and close the hinge-lock top.

4. Refrigerate the bottles, checking for fizz in about 5 days. You may have to release some fizz if you store it for more than 2 weeks. Serve chilled.

CHAPTER 10:

Foraging Nuts

While we *are* nuts for wild food foraging, I am actually referring to going out and gathering nuts to eat. I'll be discussing nuts in culinary terms as the large, edible kernels found within a tough shell and growing on trees as a means of reproduction. Collecting the nuts can seem like child's play compared to cracking the hard shells of some of them, and it is an activity we save for the cold winters when we are stuck indoors. In some years, nut trees produce amazing crops of nuts, covering the ground with hard shelled nuts, while on other years the crop is scarce, sometimes even non-existent. The trees seem to go through cycles that can be observed and tracked in anticipation of a good harvest, although weather greatly affects a tree's production. However, not all of the trees are on the same place in the cycle, so there are always nuts to be found, even if you have to search a little harder.

There are several nut trees native to North America that are important to both humans and wildlife, and historically Native Americans ate nuts as a nutritionally dense food. Nuts generally have high oil content and are rich in essential amino acids, making them a great source of energy. Their fats are the unsaturated kinds, and consumers of nuts are less likely to suffer heart disease. Many nuts also contain protein, folate, fiber, and minerals such as magnesium, phosphorus, potassium, and selenium. Unfortunately, due to their high oil content, nuts can easily go rancid, and are best roasted or frozen to preserve their goodness.

Besides excellent nutrition, there are other reasons to go nut hunting. One reason is that they taste wonderful! We add nuts to baked goods, pancakes, cookies, and muffins, as well as grind the nuts for meal to use in recipes. Many of the wild nuts you can forage are not commercially available, so you can experience new and truly local flavors. Gathering your own nuts can save you some money on your grocery bill, considering how much cultivated or commercially farmed nuts cost.

The biggest reason to hunt and collect nuts for us is that they are ready for harvest in the fall, our favorite time of the year. Our New England hardwood forests are lovely in fall with their changing colors, crisp air, and perfect temperatures. Observing the frantic squirrels and chipmunks as they forage for their winter storage is a fun activity, and the three of us gathering a gallon of acorns or hickory nuts will hardly make an impact in the available wild nuts for the animals. There is so much bounty to be had in fall between the mushrooms, nuts, and fruits like apples and cranberries that we find ourselves outside every weekend and during the week after school and work, searching for tasty edibles.

Nuts can be collected in large quantities in buckets or cloth bags, and are relatively easy to identify by examining the nut and trying to identify the tree from which it fell.

✓ Look at the shell of the nut; is it smooth or have deep ridges? Is there a green, fibrous husk on the outside, spines, or a cap?

✓ Examine the trees and use leaves and bark descriptions to try to identify the trees; some species of nut trees produce tastier nuts than others.
✓ Look for holes or cracked nuts and discard them; the holes mean the nut is infested with grubs and cracked nuts are often bad or old.
✓ Plan on processing nuts in a timely manner, as they can become rancid or moldy quickly.

Acorns N

Quercus species

Your parents might have warned you that acorns are poisonous when you were a kid and that only squirrels can eat them, but it turns out acorns are edible and can be delicious with proper preparation to remove the tannins. Acorn meal was a major part of the Native American's diet, and can be a good addition to any foraging family's diet as well.

Leaves from the red or black oak family have pointed lobes and often rather tannnic acorns that require longer soaking

How to Identify

Acorns are produced by oak trees. The leaves of different oak tree species are highly variable, but they all grow alternately and are tough and leathery. Oak leaves are usually deeply lobed, but some species have pointed, holly-like leaves. Leaves that have rounded lobes are commonly considered part of the white oak group, while leaves that have sharply pointed lobes are considered part of the red or black oak group. Oak trees produce both dangling male catkins and tiny female flowers on the same tree. Acorns have a smooth, somewhat pliable shell when fresh that will get harder as the acorn dries, and vary in shape and size between species; sometimes squat and round, other times looking like an elongated bullet, but always with a nipple-like point at its end. Acorns grow in a scaly or bristly detachable cup, also called the cap, which kids like to use for various craft projects or as bowls in fairy houses. The nut meat can vary in color from creamy white to yellow, orange, or even light purple; the meat is covered by a thin skin that should be removed, and often breaks into two halves once shelled. The tannin levels of different species of acorns varies from 3-30 percent, and the tannins must be removed to make the acorn safe to eat and palatable.

Leaves from the white oak family have rounded lobes and often sweeter acorns
that require less processing

Habitat and Range

There are approximately 90 native species of oaks in North America, all of which produce edible acorns. They can grow in many habitats such as swamps, lowland forests, rocky ridges, canyons, coastal plains, and in well drained soils. Collecting acorns from oaks will not impact their population since a single tree can produce many nuts in a good year. Turkeys, wild pigs, and small rodents like squirrels and chipmunks all consume acorns, but will not be affected by harvest of a few gallons of nuts by foraging humans.

When and How to Harvest

In good years, it may seem like acorns are covering the ground, accumulating in street gutters and at the bottoms of hills in autumn. Oak trees produce large crops in cycles, often based on weather conditions when the flowers open in spring. Fortunately, there are always some acorns in another location since all the trees may not be on the same crop cycle. Collect acorns into a bucket or cloth sack, examining them for insect and grub infestation, obvious mold, or dying sprouts.

Acorn flour made from cold leached white oak acorns

Acorns with their caps still attached are usually bad, since the tree rejected them because of insect infestation, and fresh acorns that float in a bucket of water will have grubs inside that have eaten the nut and made the nut lighter. White oak acorns sprout soon after falling in the autumn, and the acorns with healthy sprouts are fine to collect if you plan on processing the meat very soon after collection.

Eating and Preserving

Acorns can be cracked open fresh or dried and stored to crack open later. They should not be left in a bucket and forgotten about, or you will find they have molded or gone rancid, or you'll see all of the grubs that have chewed their way out of the acorns in the bottom of the bucket. We crack our acorns fresh, very soon after harvest, and they are easier to remove from the shell if they are heated for about 5 minutes in a hot oven before cracking. Robert uses a knife to cut and peel the shell, but you can crack the acorn with a nutcracker, hammer, or stone to smash open the shell and pick the meat out.

Once the meat is removed from the shell, it then needs to be leached in fresh water to remove the tannins. Tannins can cause digestive and nutrition problems by binding to proteins and iron in your body, and they are very astringent, making acorns that have not been leached unpalatable. There are two methods you can use to leach the tannins from your acorns: the hot water method and the slower, cold water method.

To use the *hot water leaching* method, the shelled acorn nut meat should be coarsely chopped. In a large pot of water, bring the nuts to a boil and cook for about 30 minutes, and watch as the water will turn brown from the tannins. Drain the water and start again with fresh water, following this process until the water no longer changes color after boiling. While the hot leaching process uses a lot of energy, it can be accomplished in one day.

The *cold water leaching* process requires no energy use, but patience and time. The shelled nut meats should be ground coarsely then added to a non-reactive container, like a large glass jar, and covered with cold water. Shake or stir the meal and water twice a day, and drain the brown water off and replace it with clean water daily, until the water no longer changes color. This process could take 1-3 weeks, but very little of your time as you only need to drain the water once or twice a day.

Once the tannins have been removed from the acorn nut meat, drain it through a jelly bag or several layers of cheesecloth. The nut meat now needs to be ground finely, either using a food processor or mortar and pestle, and then dried slowly in a low oven, spread on a cookie sheet. The dried acorn meal can now be added to baked goods along with other flours that contain gluten for structure, or cooked and eaten like grits or porridge. The ground and dried acorn flour should be stored in the freezer in an airtight container for use all year.

Acorn Cupcakes with Wild Grape Cream Cheese Icing

Makes about 42 mini cupcakes or 2-8" round cakes

Cupcakes:

1¾ cups flour
1 teaspoon baking soda

¼ teaspoon salt
4 oz. softened butter or shortening
1 cup sugar
2 eggs
6 oz. buttermilk
1 teaspoon vanilla
¾ cup acorn flour

1. Preheat the oven to 325° and line muffin pans with papers.
2. Combine the flour, baking soda and salt in a bowl.
3. Cream together the butter or shortening with the sugar until fluffy.
4. Add the eggs one at a time, scraping down the bowl between each addition.
5. Add half of the flour mixture, mix. Add the buttermilk, mix, add the remaining flour mixture.
6. Fold in the ground acorn flour and mix until incorporated.
7. Bake 8" round for 25-35 minutes, bake cupcakes 12-18 minutes until cake is springy. Cool.

Wild Grape Cream Cheese Frosting

4 oz. softened butter
6 oz. softened cream cheese
3 cups confectioners' sugar
4 Tablespoons wild grape jam

1. Mix butter and cream cheese until smooth. Add confectioners' sugar and mix until stiff, scraping bowl.
2. Add the grape jam. You want a pretty purple frosting. If the frosting is too soft, add more confectioners' sugar to help it stiffen. Chill the frosting before frosting the cupcakes, and chill the cupcakes once frosted.

Black Walnuts N

Juglans nigra

Much more strongly flavored than commercial walnuts, black walnuts are a love-them-or-hate-them nut. Collecting great quantities of nuts in autumn yields a whole winter of busy work cracking and shelling a potential bounty of gourmet nut meats for seasonal baking.

Black walnuts still in their green husks on the tree, and the de-husked nuts in their shell

How to Identify

Black walnut trees are deciduous trees that can grow to a stately 120 feet tall. They have grey, deeply furrowed bark and their twigs are smooth and brown. The compound leaves of black walnut trees grow alternately, and are 1-2 feet long, with 13-23 lance-shaped, unevenly paired leaflets that are 2-4 inches long and finely toothed. The male catkins hang below the leaf stems, while the upright female flowers are located at the tips of the branches, and once pollinated, will develop into the walnut. The walnuts are botanically the pit of the inedible green fruit, which we call the husk. The husk can be about the size of a tennis ball, and is green with a lightly pebbly surface. Inside the husk is a deeply furrowed, hard shell of the walnut, about 1½ inches in diameter containing the nut meat. When scratched, the leaves and husk of black walnut will emit a pleasant spicy/lemony odor. Black walnut trees are alleopathic, meaning they produce compounds that can inhibit the growth of other trees and plants to limit competition in their immediate area.

Habitat and Range

Black walnuts are native to North America, growing east of the Rockies throughout the Midwest and New England, south into northern Texas and Florida. They grow in rich bottomlands and floodplains in well-drained soil, but are also planted as attractive city trees and as landscaped trees. Black walnut trees are considered pioneer trees in abandoned areas, quickly growing in abandoned fields and along roadsides. They are often heavy nut producers, and the collection of a few gallons of nuts will not affect the food supply for local wildlife.

When and How to Harvest

The ripe nuts will begin to fall from the tree in the autumn, still covered by the green husk. The husk needs to be removed as soon as possible, before they become maggot infested or liquefy into black goo, and it can be a messy job, staining your hands and clothes with a dark yellow-brown color for weeks if you don't wear gloves. If the nuts have fallen on a hard surface, you can stomp on the husk to remove it, or smash it off with a flat rock. Some people like to drive over the walnuts that fall in their driveway, but doing so may produce cracks in the shell and damage the nut meat. Once the husks have been removed, we wash our nuts in a bucket of water, tossing out the nuts that float, and scrubbing them with a wire brush to remove more bits of the husk. We then let the nuts dry in a single layer for a few weeks before shelling them. Sometimes in the early summer, there is a good windstorm or heavy rain that will knock a bunch of immature walnuts off the tree outside our apartment; they are young enough that the nut shell has not hardened yet and we can slice through the whole nut with a knife. These fragrant and flavorful immature nuts can be collected and used to make homemade *nocino*, an Italian walnut liqueur, by infusing the nuts in hard alcohol.

Eating and Preserving

I'll admit that I don't like the flavor of plain black walnuts, but I think they shine in baked goods. Cracking black walnuts may be the largest obstacle left before you can start making cookies, ice cream, brownies, or muffins with your wild harvest. The shell of black walnuts is exceptionally hard, and there are several specialized and pricey nut crackers made specifically for them. Gillian enjoys using one that some fellow foraging friends have at their home, cracking and eating the assorted nuts they keep in a basket nearby. We use a hammer and nut-pick to get our prizes and it may take a bit of practice before you determine the best position to hold the nut before cracking it open. We keep the shelled nut meats in the freezer, since they contain high levels of unsaturated fats and spoil quickly. The dried, unshelled nuts can be kept for several months in a dry, dark place, letting you shell them at your leisure during the cold winter months when you are probably stuck inside anyways.

Chestnuts N, I

Castanea dentata, Castanea mollissima, Castanea pumila

Did you know that you can find your own chestnuts to roast on an open fire out in the wild? While most of the native chestnuts of North America were wiped out, introduced Chinese chestnuts and native chinquapins are equally edible and tasty substitutes.

Chestnuts in the spiny hull on the tree, and after they have ripened and fallen

How to Identify

American chestnut trees (*Castanea dentata*) and Chinese chestnut trees (*Castanea molissima*) appear very similar at first glance. They can grow from 60-100 feet tall, and both have deciduous, alternate leaves with toothed edges. Both trees produce dangling flower catkins in spring that smell very strongly, and sharply spiny nut burrs that hold 2-4 nuts in the fall. American chestnut trees have smooth twig tips that are brown, leaves that are deeply toothed with curved hook-like teeth, are 5-8 inches long, and with hairs only on the leaf midrib. The nuts are ½-1 inch wide with a pointed tip. Chinese chestnut trees have fuzzy twig tips that are greyish-tan, leaves with shallow, non-hooked teeth that are 4-8 inches long and hairy on the undersides. The nuts of Chinese chestnuts are ¾-2 inches wide with a tufted tip. Chinquapins (*Castanea pumila*) grow more like a shrub or small tree, 6-24 feet tall. Its leaves are 2-6 inches long, finely hairy on the underside, and toothed. Its catkins are erect and attached to the bases of leaves, and mature into a spiny burr containing a single nut. The nuts of these three chestnuts are considered "sweet" and are all equally edible. *Note:* Horse chestnuts (*Aesculus hippocastanum*) are a poisonous nut that some people may confuse with edible chestnuts. They have large, palmate leaves, and erect, showy flowers in spring, and the outer husk of the nut is sparsely thorny and divides into three parts when it opens to reveal a single nut that resembles edible chestnuts. Ohio buckeyes (*Aesculus glabra*) are also poisonous. Look for the spiny burrs on the ground when collecting nuts to make sure you have the edible chestnuts.

Habitat and Range

The native North American chestnut was the dominant tree in the eastern United States until the late 1800's. It was decimated by a fungal blight in that was introduced with the importation of Chinese chestnut trees that were naturally resistant to the fungus. American chestnut trees still exist in their historical range from Maine through the

Appalachian Mountains and Ohio Valley south into Mississippi, but often succumb to the fungus before they can mature enough to bear nuts. There are programs to try to breed fungus-resistant American chestnut trees for commerce that hope to bring the chestnut back into the natural landscape, and there are pockets of American chestnuts that are not affected by the fungal blight outside of their natural range. Most of the nut-bearing chestnut trees you may find are the introduced Chinese chestnuts, and they are now naturalized throughout the same areas that our native chestnut once thrived in. The native chinquapins grow east from Texas into New York and all along the east coast of North America. Chestnut tree species will readily interbreed with each other. Chestnut trees prefer full sun and rich soil, but due to their spiny burrs, do not make good landscape plantings. The nuts are important food sources for wildlife like deer, turkeys, and bears, but gathering some of the nuts for your own use should not affect the availability of food for foraging animals.

When and How to Harvest

Chestnuts ripen in the fall. The spiny burrs will split open and sometimes drop the nuts to the ground, or the whole burr will fall and you can try to get the nuts out by stepping on the burr with tough-soled shoes to open it. We sometimes use the telescoping hook to knock the

Mousse made from pureed Chinese chestnuts and cream

nuts from the higher branches of Chinese chestnut trees, but have to be careful of the falling spiny burrs! We also wear heavy duty gloves to pick up the burrs if we can't get the nuts out, and use scissors to open them at home. If you are polite and brave, you might try to knock on the door of a house with a chestnut tree in the yard and ask if you can collect the nuts. Offer to clean up some of the spiny burrs, and chances are the homeowners will be happy to share.

Eating and Preserving

We don't have a fireplace or access to an open fire, but roasting chestnuts is the traditional preparation. Use a knife to score an X on the nut shell, and slowly roast them until browned and they smell delicious. Cut off the shell while it is still warm, and try to peel the skin off of the nut before eating them whole. We boil our chestnuts for 20 minutes or so, then peel them and eat them warm. Gillian can eat them as fast as we can peel them, so sometimes I don't get too many to use for recipes like mousse, in savory stuffing, grain pilafs, and in hearty fall soups. Chestnuts have very little fat and are high in carbohydrates, and taste starchy and mildly sweet. Once cooked, shelled, and peeled, we keep them in the freezer to use all year.

Hickory Nuts N

Carya species

Crisp autumn afternoons are perfect times to gather buckets of fallen hickory nuts with the kids. These wild cousins of pecans can be collected in large amounts in good years, and provide delicious nuts for baking and snacking once shelled during the cold winter months.

How to Identify

Hickories are deciduous, native trees with pinnately compound leaves and large nuts enclosed in a four-parted, smooth green husk. The male flowers appear as long stalked catkins and female flowers as shorter

Hickory nuts in their smooth green husk

spikes at the axils of the previous season's leaves. Shagbark hickory (*Carya ovata*) grows well over 100 feet tall and mature trees have excessively shaggy bark that pulls away from the trunk in vertical strips over a foot long. The leaves are 12-24 inches long, compound with 5-7 leaflets. The nuts are enclosed in a very thick, green husk that opens to drop the ripe nuts. Shellbark hickory (*Carya laciniosa*) has grey, shaggy bark, appearing similar to shagbark hickory. The leaves are compound, up to 28 inches long with 5-9 leaflets that are lightly fuzzy on the undersides. Shellbark hickories produce large nuts up to 2 inches long in green husks that turn brown before opening and dropping the nuts. Pignut hickory (*Carya glabra*) has smooth bark, compound leaves with 5 leaflets, and the nut is covered in a thin green husk that opens to drop the nuts. Pecan trees (*Carya illinoinensis*) have flaky grey bark, compound leaves with 9-17 leaflets, and the green hull dries to brown before opening and dropping its elongated, oval nut.

Habitat and Range

The shagbark hickories grow from the Dakotas south to Texas and throughout the Eastern United States, but are absent from the lower south. Shellbark hickories grow from Kansas east to New York, south into Texas and Georgia, and all along the east coast. Pignut hickories occupy the Ohio River Basin and the Appalachian forests, south to

Florida and the east coast. Pecans grow with a more southern distribution, from Kansas south to Texas, and east to Virginia. Hickories
prefer dry, rich, mixed hardwood forests and full sun, and can live up
to 300 years. They can be found at field edges, often at old farmsteads,
and open woods. There are several other hickory tree species that are
native to North America, but many of their nuts are too bitter to eat.
Hickories will not produce a consistently heavy crop every year, but
when the nuts are abundant, collecting a few gallons for personal use
will not affect the trees or the wildlife that eat them.

When and How to Harvest

The nuts of wild hickories ripen and fall in mid-autumn, usually
around late September or the first three weeks of October. In good
years, you will see the split husks and nuts littering the ground from
far away, and can easily collect a good amount of nuts into buckets
or bags to take home. If the green husks are still closed and attached,
they can still be collected and allowed to dry in a safe place (away
from squirrels!) until the husks will split open and fall away from the
nut. The nuts are easiest to crack open with a hammer, then use a pick
to extract the nutmeat. Woodchips from cut hickories can be used to
smoke meats and cheeses.

Rugelach made with hickory nuts and dried beach plums

Eating and Preserving

Once collected, the nuts can be dried in the shell and kept uncracked for about a year. The high oil content of hickory nuts will cause them to go rancid quickly once cracked, so the shelled nuts should be kept in the freezer. I love hickory nuts, having eaten many of them as a child where there was shagbark trees growing near the house for easy nut collection. They have a rich, sweet flavor similar to pecans and walnuts, with slightly smaller nutmeats. We add them to many baked goods like muffins and coffee cakes, in homemade granola, and eat them toasted by the handful. Cracking open hickory nuts is a wintertime activity for us, using the sidewalk outside for cracking open nuts on a mild day and picking the cracked nuts while watching movies on the couch.

CHAPTER 11:

Seasonal Checklists

Knowing where to look for wild edible foods is very important, as well as knowing *when* to find them. More specifically, some plants have several different parts that are edible during different seasons, and others become too tough later in the year or die back during the heat of summer to re-emerge young and tender again in the cooler autumn months. Other plants like the lemony, tender green wood sorrel can be found during the entire growing season.

One example of a plant with seasonal edible parts would be common milkweed. In the spring, we search for and collect the young shoots, followed by the unopened flower buds and opened flower clusters in the spring, and ending with the immature seed pods in the late summer. Trying to collect the seed pods in the autumn will leave you with dry, inedible pods filled with the mature seeds and fluff that is attached to the seeds to help them catch breezes and spread.

We can't stress how beneficial and important it is to observe wild edibles through all of their seasons and stages of life. From shoots, through flowering into maturity, and going into dormancy for the winter if a perennial, or dying back completely if an annual, learning about the complete life cycle of wild edible plants helps increase understanding of the cycles of life all around us.

Different regions of North America have different climates, so these lists are approximate and will need to be adjusted accordingly to your specific region.

Spring Foraging Checklist, April through Mid-June

☐ bamboo shoots
☐ birch twigs
☐ bittercress
☐ black locust flowers
☐ burdock roots
☐ cattail pollen
☐ cattail-on-the-cob
☐ cattail shoot
☐ chickweed
☐ dandelion flowers
☐ dandelion leaves
☐ daylily shoots
☐ daylily tubers
☐ field garlic
☐ garlic mustard flower buds
☐ garlic mustard leaves
☐ garlic mustard roots
☐ grape leaves

☐ grape tendrils
☐ Japanese knotweed shoots
☐ lamb's quarters
☐ linden leaves
☐ milkweed flower buds
☐ milkweed shoots
☐ mulberry leaves
☐ nettles
☐ purslane
☐ ramps leaves
☐ sassafras leaves
☐ sassafras roots
☐ sheep sorrel
☐ spicebush twigs
☐ violet flowers
☐ violet leaves
☐ wintergreen
☐ wood sorrel

Summer Foraging Checklist, late June through August

- ☐ bayberry leaves
- ☐ beach plums
- ☐ birch twigs
- ☐ black cherries
- ☐ black raspberries
- ☐ blackberries
- ☐ blueberries
- ☐ burdock flower stalks
- ☐ cattail pollen
- ☐ cattail-on-the-cob
- ☐ choke cherries
- ☐ common mallow
- ☐ dandelion flowers
- ☐ daylily flowers
- ☐ garlic mustard leaves
- ☐ garlic mustard roots
- ☐ garlic mustard seeds
- ☐ grape tendrils
- ☐ huckleberries
- ☐ Indian cucumber
- ☐ lamb's quarters
- ☐ linden bracts
- ☐ milkweed flower buds
- ☐ milkweed pods
- ☐ mulberries
- ☐ pineapple weed
- ☐ purslane
- ☐ raspberries
- ☐ red clover
- ☐ sassafras leaves
- ☐ sassafras roots
- ☐ sheep sorrel
- ☐ strawberries
- ☐ sumac berries
- ☐ wineberries
- ☐ wintergreen leaves
- ☐ wood sorrel

Autumn Foraging Checklist, September through November

- ☐ acorns
- ☐ apples
- ☐ autumn olives
- ☐ bayberries
- ☐ bayberry leaves
- ☐ beach plums
- ☐ birch twigs
- ☐ black walnuts
- ☐ burdock roots
- ☐ chestnuts
- ☐ chickweed
- ☐ common mallow
- ☐ crabapples
- ☐ cranberries
- ☐ dandelion flowers
- ☐ dandelion roots
- ☐ daylily tubers
- ☐ garlic mustard leaves
- ☐ garlic mustard roots
- ☐ ginkgo nuts
- ☐ grapes
- ☐ hickory nuts
- ☐ pears
- ☐ purslane
- ☐ sassafras roots
- ☐ spicebush berries
- ☐ sumac berries
- ☐ wintergreen berries
- ☐ wintergreen leaves
- ☐ wood sorrel

CHAPTER 12:

Glossary of Terms

Achenes: a dry, single seeded fruit commonly mistaken for a seed; like the "seeds" of strawberries or rosehips

Aggregate fruit: a fruit that is produced from a cluster of ovaries that were separate in a single flower that fuses into a single mass; like a raspberry

Alleopathic: the ability of a plant to inhibit the growth and reproduction of other plants by producing biochemical compounds

Alternate leaf attachment: leaves that grow from opposite sides of a stalk from different points, not paired

Basal rosette: a group of leaves growing in a circular manner from their point of attachment directly to the roots

Biennial: a plant that has a two year life cycle; the first year is spent growing and collecting energy, the second year a flower stalk is produced to disperse seeds, after which the plant dies

Blanch: a cooking method to briefly boil a vegetable before plunging it into ice water to stop the cooking process; blanching retains nutrients and bright colors of vegetables before they are cooked further or frozen for preservation

Bract: a small modified leaf found beneath a flower or flower cluster

Bulb: a modified rootstock that is used by the plant to store energy; like an onion

Calyx: sepals, or the outermost cuplike parts of floral parts; these parts sometimes remain attached to the fruit of a plant

Cambium: a layer of tissue between the inner bark and wood of a tree trunk; it is the origin of growth of trees and forms the rings

Catkin: a spike of petal-less flowers

Chaff: the inedible husks of grains and grasses

Compound leaves: leaves that consist of several smaller leaflets attached to a singular stalk

Coniferous: pertaining to conifers; evergreen trees or shrubs that bear cones; like pine trees, spruce trees, yews

Corm: an enlarged bulblike base of a stem used in the same manner as a root to store energy for a plant

Cotyledon: the first leaves to emerge from a seed, they often don't look like the mature leaves and can be eaten as sprouts

Deciduous: trees that shed their leaves every year; like oaks, maples, hickory trees

Drupe: a fruit with pulp surrounding a single seed with a hard shell

Elliptic: an oval shaped leaf with a small or absent point

Endangered plant: a species of plant whose population is at risk of extinction due to human activity, climate change, or disappearance of environment; endangered species of plants should never be collected

Ephemeral: a plant with a brief growing season; ephemerals usually grow in early spring before dying back before the summer starts; ephemerals take advantage of light conditions before the upper forest story leafs out

Float test: placing nuts in water to see if they are good; generally good nuts sink and bad nuts (with bugs or poor development) will float and should be discarded

Floret: a small flower; one of many small flowers of a composite cluster

Glabrous: a smooth surface lacking hairs

Herbaceous: having no woody tissues, but tender stems; pertaining to herbs

Invasive plant: a species of plant not native to an area that has a tendency to spread and cause damage due to excessive seeding, lack of natural predators or limiting factors, and the ability to outcompete native plants for resources; invasive edible plants can be collected in large numbers, but care should be taken to not spread the plant further

IQF: stands for **I**ndividually **Q**uick **F**rozen; a method used to preserve tender or fragile foods by spreading them into a single layer on a sheet pan and freezing, then gathering up the frozen food into a bag or container for storage; IQF keeps the individual pieces separate and easier to work with in the future; use IQF for berries

latex: a white milky sap that some plants exude when cut or scratched; some people experience a rash when exposed to latex

leaching: the process of dissolving soluble constituents in a liquid; acorns must have the tannins leached from them to make them safely edible

leaf axil: the angle between the branch and leafstalk from which it grows

leaflet: a small leaf within a compound leaf

lenticel: a small spot on the surface of a plant or tree bark that serves as a pore

lobed leaf: a blade of the leaf that is divided into protrusions but still part of the leaf; leaf lobes can be rounded or pointed

mast year: refers to a year a nut tree produces a large crop of nuts; mast is the term used for the nuts produced and dropped by a tree

midrib: the main stalk of a compound leaf; the main, sturdy vein of a simple leaf

mucilaginous: a part of a plant that produces a sticky or thickly slimy starch called mucilage

native plant: a plant that occurs naturally or has existed for many years in an area without human intervention; native plants coexist in a balance with other plants, animals, and microorganisms in an environment; collection of native plants should be limited to no more than 10-25% of an abundant population

nutlet: a small nutlike fruit or seed; the stone of a drupe; like the seeds of huckleberries

nutmeat: the edible portion of a nut

opposite leaf attachment: leaves that grow in pairs on opposite sides of a stem

Palmate: leaf arrangement from which multiple leaflets are attached at the same point to the stem; hand-shaped leaf

Perennial: a plant having a life cycle that is more than two years long; a plant that will return from its roots year after year

Petiole: stem or stalk of a leaf

Pinnately compound: leaflet arrangement along opposite sides of a midrib of a compound leaf; like a fern or black walnut leaf

Pistil: female part of a flower that bears the seed or fruit

Puree: to make the pulp of a fruit or vegetable smooth through processing; purees have stems or seeds removed by straining and can be used to make fruit leathers and soups

Raceme: a flower cluster in which flowers grow on short stems attached to a common, elongated stem; like black cherry flowers

Rhizome: underground rootstock which grows horizontal to the surface used to store the plant's energy; there are often swollen nodes and thin hair-like roots on rhizomes

Root: the underground part of a plant that stores energy, anchors the plant to the ground, and absorbs nutrients

Root crown: the part of the root from which the plant's stem arises

Sepals: part of the flowers, sometimes colored green or the same color as the flower petals, the sepals are modified leaves that form a ring beneath the flower petals

Schizocarp: a dry fruit that splits into single seeded parts, like mallow cheeses

Serrated leaves: leaves with edges that are toothed

Shoot: the stem of a plant emerging from the ground as new growth, sometimes with unfurling leaves present

Siliques: elongated seed pod of mustard plants; like garlic mustard or bittercress

Spile: wooden or metal spout used when tapping trees to collect sap for making into syrup; usually a bucket will hang from a hook on the spile to catch the sap

Stamen: the male part of a flower, bearing the pollen

Succulent: a plant with thick, fleshy, and juicy tissues

Tannin: an organic acid that imparts an astringent taste, tannins are polyphenolic compounds that should not be consumed in large amounts

Taproot: the main root of a plant growing downward, often with smaller roots attached

Tendril: a threadlike organ of climbing plants used to help the plant climb structures by coiling and to support the plant; like grape tendrils

Terminal leaflet: the leaflet at the end of a midrib or stem of a compound leaf

Tuber: the thickening of the underground stem used to store energy for a plant; like a potato

Umbel: a flower cluster in which a number of flower stalks spread from a common center

Whorled: leaf arrangement on a stem in which the leaves are arranged around a point on an axis

Winnow: the action of removing the chaff from seeds using air to blow away the lighter chaff, leaving the edible seeds or grains behind

CHAPTER 13:

Additional Resources

Books

Brill, "Wildman" Steve, and Evelyn Dean. *Identifying and Harvesting Edible and Medicinal Plants in Wild (and Not So Wild) Places.* Available via his website wildmanstevebrill.com

Haines, Arthur. *Ancestral Plants: A Primitive Skills Guide to Important Edible, Medicinal, and Useful Plants of the Northeast, Volume 1.* Available via his website arthurhaines.com

Lincoff, Gary. *The Joy of Foraging: Gary Lincoff's Illustrated Guide to Finding, Harvesting, and Enjoying a World of Wild Food* and *National Audubon Society Field Guide to North American Mushrooms.* Available via his website garylincoff.com

Tatum, Billy Joe. *Wild Foods Field Guide and Cookbook*

Thayer, Sam. *The Forager's Harvest: A Guide to Identifying, Harvesting, and Preparing Edible Wild Plants* and *Nature's Garden: A Guide to Identifying, Harvesting, and Preparing Edible Wild Plants.* Available via his website foragersharvest.com

Internet Resources and Blogs

The3foragers.blogspot.com
eattheweeds.com
fat-of-the-land.blogspot.com
honest-food.net
foragersharvest.com
wildmanstevebrill.com
garylincoff.com
arthurhaines.com
wildfoodgirl.com
wildfoodplants.com
tagyerit.com/freefood.htm
urbanoutdoorskills.com

Find Wild Food Instructors in Your Area

eattheweeds.com/foraging/foraging-instructors/

Index